GEORGE YOUNG

Teacher, Performer, War Hero, Friend.

Alan Sharp

Published by Alan Sharp
Publishing partner: Paragon Publishing, Rothersthorpe
First published 2019
© Alan Sharp 2019

ISBN 978-1-78222-693-2

Book design, layout and production management by Into Print
www.intoprint.net

+44 (0) 1604 832149

Alan Sharp attended CRGS and University College London. After National Service in the Royal Artillery, he worked in the electronics industry in production and personnel management for 13 years. Subsequently he joined the Coverdale Organisation where he was a senior consultant and then executive director. Later he worked as an independent consultant. For a number of years he visited Harvard twice a year to join the Director and staff of the Harvard Negotiation Project in running negotiation workshops. He is co-author of two books. MANAGER AND TEAM DEVELOPMENT (Heinemann 1990) and GETTING IT DONE (HarperBusiness 1998). The latter has been published in a dozen languages, including German, Spanish, Portuguese and Chinese.

CONTENTS

ACKNOWLEDGEMENTS

THIS BOOK COULD NOT HAVE been written without the contributions of very many friends of George Young. First there are all those who contributed their personal memories described in the Appendix. I am grateful to all of them, but I owe a great personal debt of gratitude to David Sowter. For without his good sense in inviting friends and former students to contribute those memories on the occasion of the celebration of George's 90th Birthday and putting them in a binder to present to George, they would not exist. Further, David and I are both grateful to George's daughter, Alison, for keeping that binder safe over the succeeding years and arranging to scan the contents and send them to us when we had the idea of producing this book. Finally on the Appendix, I am grateful to David again for editing and organising the contents.

Second, I acknowledge the help I received on the text for the various chapters and for providing many of the illustrations that accompany that text. Alison Young provided some information and the photographs for Chapter 1 – George's early life. She also provided the press cuttings for the succeeding chapters about his war time experiences. I am grateful to David Richardson and Peter Herbert for the extracts from The Colt Magazine in Chapter 6. Roderic Knott contributed information for Chapter 7 about George's part in the Eponymous and Phoenix Music Hall and other groups; Barbara Pears told me of his contribution to the Priory Players and other amateur theatre groups. Chapter 7 also contains some press reports and photographs originally published in the Colchester Evening Gazette. I am extremely grateful to Newsquest Essex for giving their consent for the use of this material. Peter Herbert provided most of the photographs for Chapter 8.

However I owe the greatest debt to Jim Acheson. Without his foresight in persuading George to record his memories for posterity, it would have been impossible to produce this book.

INTRODUCTION

GEORGE YOUNG WAS A MAN of many and varied talents. These he used to the great benefit of all those with whom he came into contact throughout a long life.

As an exceptionally gifted and effective teacher he inspired generations of students during his career. The appendix of this book includes many individuals' memories of his impact on them. In addition, more than 65 years after they first encountered him at school, former students who were proud to call themselves "Friends of George Young" initiated and ran an appeal to raise funds to go towards a continuing memorial to him at Colchester Royal Grammar School. The result is a fine building bearing his name. More than one hundred contributed to the appeal, an indication of the regard in which they held him. Yet another indication is that, well over 100 years after his birth on 28 March 1911, more than forty attend an annual lunch to celebrate his birthday. His friends find it difficult to believe that any teacher in any part of the world could exceed such a record of excellence, popularity and enduring legacy.

He was a teacher by profession. Yet his influence and contribution extended well beyond the school. As a war-time soldier he had a distinguished career on active service as an officer with the Green Howards during the 1939-45 war. His own description of his experience provides some clues of how he must have been regarded by the men under his command. As described in the Chapter on D-Day, one of them even had a part in seeing that he was awarded the Military Cross for his bravery in the fighting that followed the landing.

Outside the school, both before and after his retirement, he performed on the theatre and Music Hall stage until after his 90th birthday, receiving a national award at the age of 91 as the oldest regular amateur performer in the country. As an actor and director with a number of local drama groups he made a huge contribution to the theatrical life of Colchester. He also helped raise substantial funds to help keep the old Repertory Theatre going and assist with the establishment of the Mercury Theatre. David Forder, who was the first chief executive of that theatre, said that George's contribution to the community in Colchester was somehow greater than the sum of its parts.

In the foyer of the George Young Building there is relevant information about George. Laurie Holmes, the School Archivist, selected and placed this there. She based it on material which I and other friends assembled and passed to her. However, there was much more than could be used for her purpose. It also needed to be organised in some way if it were to be retained for posterity. I felt that one way of achieving this would be to use as much as practicable in writing this "biography" of George.

In practice, what follows could almost be described as an "autobiography", since I have used his words where possible. Possibly, the best description is as a "semi-autobiography", though we can imagine what George would have made of such a conceit. Many of George's words come from the filmed interview conducted by Jim Acheson. While much of the content of that interview is included in the text that follows, I would still encourage any reader who has not seen it to beg or borrow a copy of the DVD. It shows George at his story-telling best, and nothing can replace that experience. As with this book, those interested in the first instance are likely to be those who knew George, Nevertheless you do not need to have known George personally to enjoy his skill in telling a story, to see the historical value of his first hand descriptions of life on the front line during World War 2, to appreciate what the theatre, and teaching and friendship meant to him.

Chapter 1 is a brief description of his early life. This is based on what he said himself in the filmed interview, augmented by some facts checked with his daughter, Alison. She also provided all the photographs for this chapter.

Chapter 2 covers his call up for war service and experience in training. The photograph here was also provided by Alison.

The next three chapters describe his experiences on active service in North Africa, Sicily and Italy and on D-Day and the fighting that followed, in which George was awarded the Military Cross and received the injury which ended his active service. In these chapters I have included photocopies of press cuttings referring to actions in which the Green Howards were involved. These had been cut from the papers at the time by George's wife, Eve, and kept by George for the rest of his life. Again I am grateful to Alison for providing these. When reading them one can only imagine Eve's feelings when she knew these were actions in which George had almost certainly been risking his life.

Chapter 6 describes how he came to join Colchester Royal Grammar School in 1947 and something of his experience there from his first day until he left in 1965. It describes his contribution to the life of the school, from his running of Under 14 Cricket and Rugby to his production and direction of the school plays. It includes extracts from The Colt magazine which he wrote and produced. These come from copies which David Richardson had kept from that time and later sent to Peter Herbert. The chapter also gives an indication of George's approach to teaching.

Chapter 7 records something of George's contribution to the wider community in Colchester. The late David Forder kindly gave me a transcript of what he said at George's funeral. Roderic Knott contributed material about George's part in the Eponymous and Phoenix Music Hall and other groups. Barbara Pears told me of his contribution to the Priory Players.

Chapter 8 describes how George maintained contact for so many years as a friend of so many of those he had taught. Most of the photographs in this chapter were contributed by Peter Herbert.

Chapter 9 covers the setting up of the "Friends of George Young", the raising of funds to go towards a continuing memorial to George at CRGS and the George Young Building.

The book concludes with an Appendix comprising personal memories of George from a number of those whom he taught. They were originally gathered by David Sowter on the occasion of George's 90th Birthday in 2001 and given to George at that time. They were retained by Alison who very kindly scanned them and sent copies to David who has collated and edited them, where necessary, for this book.

1: EARLY YEARS

GEORGE YOUNG WAS BORN ON 28th March 1911 in Kent. As he described it, his life in the 1920s was full. He went to school at St. Dunstan's College in Catford, where his father was second master. There he played Rugby Football and Cricket and belonged to the Cadets. An April 1929 photograph shows him among those attending a Drill and Tactics Course for Cadet NCOs. A second photograph shows him as a Sub-Prefect at the school in 1928 and a further, later one, as a Prefect. Describing his early years to Jim Acheson, George said "It was a day school. I went to school and I went back home, and I played Rugby Football and I played Cricket. My time was full as a schoolboy. There was also the cinema, of course. My father and mother used to go every Monday evening to the cinema, and I used to go with them."

"However the most remarkable thing about my upbringing was Nellie, the maid. I was seven years younger than my next brother – I arrived rather unexpectedly, I feel. Nellie, who had come to be the maid, took a fancy to me and she looked after me. She used to take me up to London on her day off when I got a bit older, about 14 or 15. She used to take me to the theatre. While she did not take me to this, I remember I saw Othello, with Paul Robeson. That was something, I can tell you. I can see him now, all these years later. When they came to arrest him, and he came out on the steps and said 'Put up your bright swords, or the dew will rust them' He was splendid, brilliant. It was a supreme performance. There was also a chap who played Iago. He was also brilliant. The two of them were magnificent together. This chap went off to New York, and he acted a bit there. Then he married a very rich woman and went out of the business, which I always used to think was a great loss."

"Mostly, of course, with Nellie I used to go and see musical comedies, and things like that – something I've enjoyed all my life. I like music and I've always been fascinated by the Music Hall. What a wonderful thing it was. On the last day of the holidays my father and mother always used to take me up to London to the Palladium or one of the music halls. I saw many of the performers of those days. They were wonderful entertainers, and they didn't have microphones! I used to go also to the Penge Empire. When I was about 18 you could have a delightful evening out for a shilling, five pence. You paid sixpence to go in the gallery, and then you went to the pub round the corner. There you had half a pint of beer and toasted cheese for the other sixpence. Then you walked home."

Returning to his family, George added "My eldest brother was a very good rugby player. He had been in the First World War and then had a job in the Bank of England. He used to play for the Old Blues, the old boys of Christ's Hospital, and hooked for Kent. I think if he had been a bit bigger he might well have finished up as an international. He only weighed about 12 stone and there were 13 or 14 stone people around even then. It's got up to 18 stone now. Fancy being tackled by an 18 stoner! Or, what's worse, tackling an 18 stoner. By gum, you've got to know where you're putting your shoulder then."

From school George went to Jesus College, Oxford to read English. A photograph shows him as a member of Jesus College Dramatic Society in 1931. After graduating he did some supply teaching and then taught at a preparatory school in Seascale, Cumbria. It was there he met his wife-to-be, Eve, who was Matron. They married in 1938. Their daughter, Alison, was born in 1939, by which time he had moved to Blackpool Grammar School, where he taught until he was called up to serve in the war. When the war started, as a teacher he was in a reserved occupation. However after Dunkirk the age for call up was raised and he was duly called up.

LONDON DISTRICT SCHOOL OF INSTRUCTION.
Cadet N.C.O's. Drill and Tactics Course, April, 1929.

(1) Cadet N.C.O.'s Drill and Tactics Course, April 1929. (George 3rd from left in 2nd row from back)

(2) ST. DUNSTAN'S COLLEGE Sub-Prefects 1928 (George 4th from left front row)

(3) St. Dunstan's College Prefects (George 4th from left front row)

(4) JESUS COLLEGE DRAMATIC SOCIETY June 1931 (George middle of front row)

2: THE WAR YEARS – BASIC TRAINING

THE EVACUATION FROM DUNKIRK WAS at the end of May 1940. Subsequently George was called up and interviewed by a recruiting officer in Blackpool. He said "Well, you're six foot three. You could go into the Guards or you could go into the military police, or where do we send you?" George replied "Oh, well, I'll go into the Scots Guards." His mother was Scottish.

So George went down to the Scots Guards barracks in Chelsea. A December 1940 photograph shows him in a training unit there. One day, as George described it "The Queen Mother's nephew, who was my captain, Captain the Honourable J. P. Bowes-Lyon, sent for me and said, 'We've been investigating you, Young. You got the army certificates A and B when you were at the Officers' Training Corps. You know, you ought to have a commission. We'll have to think about it.' So he sent for me about three weeks later, and he said – and this is fascinating – he actually said, 'I'm afraid that I made a mistake about this. I filled in the wrong form, Young. But I filled in the right form this time, and there's no doubt that you'll be hearing something pretty soon.'"

"So off I had to go to see the colonel of the regiment. I went off, and there he was, 'Old Bugalugs' they used to call him, because he had hair growing out of his ears. We had some conversation, and then after a bit, he said 'Well, have you got a regiment you'd like to go to?' Now it so happened that before I went to see the colonel, Captain Bowes-Lyon said to me 'Have you got a couple of hundred a year of your own, Young?' I said 'Why, sir?' He said 'If you had a couple of hundred a year of your own, I would be very pleased to get you back into the Scots Guards as an ensign. But, to be quite honest, in the bar and in the mess it would be very uncomfortable for you if you didn't have enough money.' So he said he thought I should go for a line regiment."

"Now I saw that the Green Howards had had a lot of casualties, and I thought they will want some officers. So I said 'Well, I was thinking of the Green Howards, sir.' He said to his aide-de-camp 'Mmm. Charles, who are the Green Howards?' So the aide-de-camp went and got the book, and he said 'Belong to Colonel Franklin, sir' 'Oh, Colonel Franklin, know him well, Young' he said. 'Yes, I'll write today. Don't let me forget, Charles. Don't forget to salute, Young.' Don't forget to salute! Kindly man he was."

"Then I was given the instruction that I was to go up to Northumberland and report to the 11th Green Howards and that I would be an officer from the moment I arrived. However I was, of course, still dressed as a Scots Guardsman! So off I went and got there, arriving rather late at night. Next morning, I came down to breakfast in the mess, and the Commanding Officer got the shock of his life as a Scots

Guardsman walked in. He said 'Who the hell are you?' I explained and he said to the adjutant 'Bring him in at orders.' So I was shot in then and he said 'Go away, get a uniform and then come back.'

"So there I was. I had never been to an OCTU. I must be the only person who was actually given a commission without any reason whatsoever. So that was how I got there. Very charming chap, he was, the CO, I discovered afterwards. He got used to me in time. I was there, you see, in the training battalion. Anyway, I went on this course there and I didn't do badly. It got to the last week and we were firing off. I'd done very well with the rifle shooting and I was in the lead. We'd all put some money down to go to the winner, you see. I was still leading with three days to go and the pistol shot was the only thing left. The sergeant took me on one side, and he said 'You know, you're in luck. The governor is going to offer you the job of coming on here as an instructor when you've finished the course.' I thought 'This is splendid. This is alright. I'm going to be here for the duration.' " However, the next day George received his marching orders to leave the 11th Battalion and was drafted to go out to the desert in North Africa.

Incidentally it was while with the 11th that he received the name "Bolo". One day he was talking to some fellow officers in the mess and telling them that in the Scots Guards a chap was called a Bolo, a Bolshevik, if he was seen as a troublemaker. The commanding officer overheard and said "That just about describes you, BOLO". George said he was always Bolo from that time on.

Photograph showing George when in basic training (first from left in second row)

15

3: THE WAR YEARS – NORTH AFRICA

To get to North Africa George said they went first in a large ship across the Atlantic towards America and then down the coast to Brazil. While there they learned that there were submarines about. Therefore they decided to make a run for it at night and go as fast as they could across to South Africa. Eventually they got round into Durban. It had been a very long way round and they had been on the ship for a very long time. From Durban they went up into Egypt, to Alexandria to a big camp to wait to be posted to their units. He said they were there for a long time. Suddenly one night in their tents everybody started shouting "Let me out! Let me out!" George said the chap in charge of the camp was furious. He rushed around, threatening all sorts of things.

Then things began to move. George went on a train for some days to Tobruk and then onwards on a boat. They went up to a place where the great battle of Mareth was to take place. This was some time after Alamein. As he described it George was "decanted onto a patch of desert with one or two tents around". Suddenly, a young officer appeared. He was so young he looked as though he might have been the captain of the First XI at cricket. He gave George a great welcome and said "I'm one of the other junior officers in the company, and Captain Honeyman will be coming along soon." Of course, when Captain Honeyman arrived, he said, "Hello, Bolo. My God, I'm jolly glad to see you". He had been in the 11th Battalion and George had known him well there. George said "So I got an instant welcome. I was very, very lucky."

George said then he went to bed in a tent, and after a bit a voice in the darkness said "Mr. Young, sir, do you remember me?" He said, "Lance Corporal Richardson in the 11th Battalion." George said, "Oh, yes, I remember you. You're here too, are you?" He said, "Yes, sir, and there are several of us. We're jolly glad that you've come, sir. I don't want to put myself forward, but I've been at this lot for a bit now. If you come with me with my section always, then I can give you as much help as I can." George said "What a lucky bloke I was, wasn't I?"

As George said, he arrived there in the desert just before the great battle of Mareth. His battalion, the 6th Battalion were involved in the attack. It was in this battle that the commanding officer of the 7th Battalion won the Victoria Cross.

NB While George was on active service his wife, Eve, kept press cuttings about actions involving the Green Howards. This and the following chapters include photocopies of a number of these. In addition there was one, not shown here, that records that among the Green Howards injured was Young, Lieut. G. M. In view of his rank at the time this was probably early during his time in North Africa.

The Germans fell back to the Akarit line. There was another great battle there.

George described an incident that occurred while his battalion were waiting to put an attack in. He said "We were lying among some rocks and the shells were falling. I was engaged in putting big rocks, when I could find them, in front of me so that I got some protection. Suddenly the Brigadier arrived – Brigadier Cooke-Collis, Red Ted we called him. He spoke to the commanding officer of the battalion, who spoke to the company commander. I said to one of my other officers, 'It's going to be me next, isn't it?' And suddenly old Honeyman shouts, 'Bolo!' And so I went, and the commanding officer said, 'There's this anti-tank ditch in front down there. You see it?' I suppose it was about 200 yards away from where we were. He said, 'Get in there with your platoon and cover the advance of the rest.' "

"Now, he was a mad bugger, this chap. You never knew what he was going to do next. Anyway, so we started off and we walked through. I thought … Well shells were dropping. I thought, 'We're never going to get there, are we?' You know, all these shells fall and they never touch anybody. We all got into this anti-tank ditch and I lined it up, you see. We were all there with our rifles at the ready and everything. All of a sudden the commanding officer comes belting in. He said, 'You're a bloody funk, Bolo.' I said, 'Wait a minute, sir, what's all this about?' Well, he said, 'Why didn't you go on? Why didn't you go on, Young?' I said, 'Well, you told me to stay here, sir. I've got a job here. I'm going to cover the advance.' He said, 'I think you're still a bloody funk'. And he got up and he started to walk towards the enemy lines. True!"

"I started to walk behind him. He said, 'What are you doing?' I said 'Well someone will have to go back and tell Major Honeyman that he's in charge of the battalion, won't they?' And he said 'What do you mean?' Of course I didn't think I was going to last the day out in all probability anyway. So I said 'Look, sir, why don't you go back and run the game from battalion headquarters?' He gave me a look and he went off. Well, we had this battle, and in it my life was saved in a most remarkable way. We put in an attack and we got the opposition dealt with, at least so I thought. But I was in position on the hillside, and I could see the German army in the plain below. So I thought 'We must get an artillery officer up to have a look and give the Germans a bit of stick. And so I started off to run back to where I could get a message through. Then a couple of snipers had a go at me. I hit the deck, luckily, and rolled away to one side, and then jumped up and went about ten paces zig-zag and went down again. I repeated this several times until I managed to get a message through to get an artillery officer up. At the end of the day when I took my haversack off my back, one of those bullets that the snipers had shot at me had gone through the haversack, through my mess tin, through a tin of bully beef and was just resting on my back. Amazing isn't it? It would have killed me, wouldn't it?"

After this action George was sent to Tobruk with some men to lay out a big camp for the division when they arrived. After they arrived he was sent for again and told that all the troops would be going on the train from Tobruk but that he would have the divisional commander's jeep and be in charge of the divisional transport until he delivered them in Alexandria. He said it took a good few days to get there. The last night before they reached Alexandria there was a NAAFI there. He said "After all this there was a NAAFI serving food. And so I summoned them all. Now, the law was that you had to look after your vehicles directly you got in. You had to check everything before you did anything else. I said, 'Look. There will be lots of other people getting in there. Play the game with me. Don't do your cleaning up now. All of you get off into the Naafi and get something to eat and then come back.' I said, 'Then we'll do it afterwards. Play the game.' And I said, 'When you come back, do tidy yourselves up if you can, you know, because we'll be going to Alex tomorrow.' And so there was this wonderful sight after they got back. Chaps were stark naked except for their boots. They'd all washed. They were all hanging out to dry as they did their jobs. The next morning, of course, standing up in my jeep, holding onto the front, we went through the streets of Alexandria."

YORKSHIRE TROOPS TO THE FORE

Gallant Story of First Assault on the Mareth Line

By a Front Line Observer

FEW infantry regiments have seen more bitter fighting in this war than the battalions of the Green Howards, the East Yorkshire Regiment and the Durham Light Infantry which form part of the 50th (Northumbrian) Division serving with the Eighth Army. It was this division which broke clean through the defences of the Mareth Line and held the bridgehead grimly for 48 hours before withdrawing.

The selection of the 50th Division for this assault was appropriate enough for they were the first infantry division to reach the North African battlefield from England two years ago. They have fought from El Alamein to Mareth and had enhanced their fighting tradition in many of the battles which preceded the final forward sweep. These men from Yorkshire, Durham and Northumberland—men who before the war served in the Territorial Army—were set a formidable twofold task.

ATTACK AT NIGHT

First, the enemy was to be driven from outposts about 5,000 yards in front of the Mareth Line. Second, the main line, with its concrete pillboxes and deep trenches made by the French in 1936, its anti-tank ditch, its minefields and steep and muddy Wadi Zigzaou, was to be broken.

On the nights March 16-17 and 17-18, men of the Green Howards and the East Yorkshire Regiment made a series of attacks which forced the enemy back from the outposts. These were protected by a screen of minefields which were not marked. A hitch would have gravely prejudiced the timing for the main attack, but the attacks were carried out with clockwork precision, and on March 18 our foremost troops were within 1,000 yards of the notorious Wadi Zigzaou and for the first time troops of the Eighth Army were able to observe directly the coastal end of the famous Mareth Line.

The division then faced the supreme task, timed for March 20. There were pillboxes and barbed wire beyond the further bank of the wadi, and mines and a 150 wide stream in the bed of sappers went to work like blacks. There were steep banks on either side. When the check was emptied crossing place, but the sappers continued on the night of March 20-21, patrols had already measured the width and depth of the anti-tank ditch, measured the height of the wadi banks, and gained a shrewd idea of the lay-out of the enemy defences. All this under the nose and the guns of the enemy.

THE GREEN HOWARDS

At 10.15 hrs, covered by a barrage which German prisoners subsequently described as "worse than anything at Stalingrad," the 50th Division assaulted the Mareth Line. First the Green Howards attacked a position protected by an anti-tank ditch and mines, which constituted part of the main Mareth defences. Its capture was essential to the success of the main attack. The Green Howards advanced through a storm of shelling and mortar fire, carrying small scaling ladders to help them over the anti-tank ditch. The battalion was led by small fighting patrols whose job it was to advance close under the artillery barrage, clear mines and overwhelm machinegun nests before the main bodies arrived. These tough infantrymen blazed the trail for those behind, and spread terror among the enemy.

The Commanding Officer helped to place the first scaling ladder in position, and was first over the anti-tank ditch. A hand-to-hand struggle with Germans then ensued. Two incidents stand out. The artillery fired smoke. The battalion commander, with another officer, groped his way forward through the smoke and found a cavity where the enemy were still in possession. He borrowed a grenade, threw it into the trench, and 49 Germans surrendered. No wonder the Green Howards say "They have no stomach for fighting when we get close to them."

About this time a company clerk was standing with one or two officers in the battle area. He had an "office manner," and when he saw a group of Germans in a trench in front of him he said "Excuse me, gentlemen," before calmly walking between the officers, advancing on the trench and throwing a grenade into it. The objective was gained.

DURHAM MEN

Daylight brought the inevitable counterattacks, which were all beaten back with heavy losses to the enemy, and a German sniper was shot from his perch in a palm tree. Meanwhile, the main attack was delivered. Men of the Durham Light Infantry moved towards the wadi. Shells, mortar bombs and machine-gun bullets were raining among the advancing infantry. They kept steadfastly on, crossed the wadi, and, turning left and right, stormed the strongholds of Kasba Ouen and Ouerzi with the bayonet.

The Eighth Army had gained a footing on the Mareth Line. The immediate task was to clear a crossing of the wadi for tanks and transport, and bridge the stream. The divisional guns of Mareth pounded the narrow crossing place, but the sappers continued to work. "Work was extremely difficult for the sappers," says a terse official report. It was indeed, with machine-guns firing straight down the wadi at them and shells whistling to earth about them.

By first light only four tanks had been able to get across to support the Durhams, but the full moral effect of this terrific frontal assault was seen during the day, when there was no attempt at counter-attack and the greater part of the garrisons at the strongholds of Kasba Ouen and Ouerzi Ouen surrendered.

By night the Durhams attacked again. The crossing was improved and tanks managed to get over, but their passage churned up the mud and anti-tank guns could not be got across in any numbers.

A CRUCIAL STEP

On March 22 the enemy was obliged to take a step which may have exercised a prolonged influence on the battle elsewhere. He decided to commit his armoured forces and reserve infantry to battle in that sector. In the thick palm groves of Zarat the enemy tanks formed up, then moved on our positions, in company with infantry.

The forces in the bridgehead, both tanks and infantry, virtually cut off from reinforcement by the bad condition of the only crossing, fought their lonely battle throughout the afternoon, when darkness fell our remaining forces were still fighting doggedly from the anti-tank ditch. They had their backs to the wadi, and were hanging on by the skin of their teeth to the last few yards of the bridgehead. They made the anti-tank ditch their last ditch, and the graves along the length to-day bear witness to their devotion.

At one period the enemy got behind them. A private soldier organised and led the charge with fixed bayonets that routed them. Men with Bren carriers carried the dangerous wadi crossing to bring back ammunition; one carrier managed to tow over a sorely needed anti-tank gun in the face of fierce enemy fire.

THE WITHDRAWAL

These sorely tried men, and the defenders of Kasba Ouen—who were still in possession of that strongpoint—hung on until the early hours, and at 01.30 hours, with the aid of magnificent artillery and medium machinegun support, they repulsed a heavy attack. Not until the night of March 23-24 did the enemy regain full control of the bridgehead. Our garrison withdrew when bigger plans made their gallant resistance of no further advantage.

That is the story of how the "Fifty Div."—as it is commonly known in the Eighth Army—drove a hole into what has been described as a miniature Maginot Line," and dealt the first of the heavy blows that sent the enemy limping to the north.

GREEN HOWARDS

How They Captured and Held a Vital Position

From a Military Correspondent

THE GREEN HOWARDS (Alexandra, Princess of Wales's Own Yorkshire Regiment), the old 19th Foot, and the first regiment to be raised in England for William of Orange, have been famous throughout modern British military history. Their gallant service of 1914-18 has been paralleled by equally fine work in the present war, especially in the North African campaign.

On the night of March 20-21 last, the task of a battalion of the Green Howards was to attack and capture an important feature on the left flank of the main attack on the Mareth Line. The defence of this feature was very strong, and it was protected by an anti-tank ditch 12 feet wide and eight feet deep, with minefields on both sides. It formed a new part of the main defences of the Mareth Line and the successful capture of this feature was vital to the success of the main attack.

From the time the attack was launched the battalion was subjected to the most intense fire from artillery, machine-guns and mortars, and it appeared more than probable that the battalion would be held up, entailing failure of the main attack.

ENEMY WIPED OUT

Realising the seriousness of the situation, Lieutenant-Colonel Derek Anthony Seagrim, whose home is at Westward Ho, Devon, placed himself at the head of his battalion, which was, at the time, suffering heavy casualties, and led it through the hail of fire.

He personally helped the team which was placing the scaling ladder over the anti-tank ditch and was himself the first to cross it. He led the assault firing his pistol, throwing grenades and assaulting two machine-gun posts which were holding up the advance of one of his companies. It is estimated that in this phase he killed or captured 20 Germans.

His display of leadership and personal courage led directly to the capture of the objective.

When dawn broke the battalion was firmly established on the position, which was of obvious importance to the enemy, who immediately made every effort to regain it. Every post was mortared and machine-gunned unmercifully, and movement became almost impossible, but Lieut.-Colonel Seagrim was undeterred. He moved from post to post, organising and directing the fire until the attackers were wiped out to a man.

By his valour, disregard for personal safety and outstanding example, he so inspired his men that the battalion successfully took and held its objective, thereby allowing the attack to proceed.

Lieut.-Colonel Seagrim subsequently died of wounds received in action. He was awarded the V.C. posthumously.

Nine months earlier the Green Howards had burst their way through the encircling Germans at Mersa Matruh, only a couple of weeks after the famous counter-attack and desert march in the withdrawal from Gazala.

"It was already dark," runs the account of the Mersa Matruh fighting given by Private P. Day, of Benwell, Newcastle-upon-Tyne, "when the order came to get ready to smash through the Jerries, who had got round our flank and out on the road behind us.

"We had already served the same trick on the Hun back at Gazala, so we reasoned ourselves pretty good at it. Then, the Hun had been so scared when our lorries came racing towards them out of the darkness over slit trenches, and all that many of them tried to climb aboard our trucks in their eagerness to surrender and we had to beat at their knuckles with our rifle butts to make them drop off. Of course we did not expect Jerry to behave quite like that, but we were all set to give him a jolt and disappoint his hopes of putting us in the bag.

BLAZING TRUCKS

"We piled into our trucks with our Brens, Tommy-guns and rifles all ready for the business. This time we were going to blaze away as we went through—at Gazala we had been told not to fire if possible, in order to conceal our movement.

"We sat there in the dark, waiting for the final order to get going, while Jerry tracer-bullets and shells weaved patterns in the sky.

"At last we got the word 'Go,' and off we shot. Jerry was on a ridge to our right, and he let rip at us as soon as he twigged what was happening. As we lurched and bounded along we blazed back at him with everything we had.

"Several trucks were hit by anti-tank shells and caught fire, acting as torches to light up the scene for the Jerry-gunners. Most of the boys in them were able to jump out and climb into other trucks till they were packed like sardines. The whole sky seemed to be criss-crossed with tracer and lit up with flares, but we hadn't time to stop and admire the view, as you can imagine.

"At last we were out of the ring of fire. We had got over the first and worst hurdle, but we were still a long way from home. The enemy was across the road for a long way about, and it would have been suicide to go racing down it in a column. So we made off into the desert, which sure too had going in those parts. Of course, we mostly got split up in the darkness—it was a case of every man, or rather every truck best, for himself.

NORWAY AND FRANCE

The 1st Battalion of the Green Howards took part in the Norwegian campaign and on April 19, 1940, put up a particularly stubborn resistance to the Germans at Otta. Other units of the Regiment formed part of the 23rd Division, which fought in France and Belgium in May, 1940, and retired through Dunkirk.

They had as many as 24 battalions in the last war, when 12 Victoria Crosses were won by members of the Regiment.

TWO NEW VCs – POSTHUMOUS AWARD TO MARETH HERO

TWO NEW V.C.s: POSTHUMOUS AWARD TO MARETH HERO

THE King has approved the posthumous award of the Victoria Cross to Major (Temp. Lt.-Col.) Derek Anthony Seagrim, the Green Howards.

Lieut.-Col. Seagrim, whose home is at Westward Ho, Devon, led his battalion through a hail of fire in the attack on the Mareth Line, personally assaulted two machine-gun posts and killed or captured 20 Germans. He died later of wounds received in action.

A second V.C. goes to Naviidar Parkash Singh, 8th Punjab Regiment, Indian Army, for "very gallant actions" in Burma, where, under heavy fire, he rescued the crews of carriers which had been put out of action.

Describing Lieut.-Col. Seagrim's heroism the citation says:

"On the night of March 20-21, 1943, the task of a battalion of the Green Howards was to attack and capture an important feature on the left flank of the main attack on the Mareth Line.

"The defence of this feature was very strong. It was protected by an anti-tank ditch 12ft. wide and eight feet deep with minefields on both sides.

"From the time the attack was launched the battalion was subjected to the most intense fire from artillery, machine-guns and mortars.

"Realising the seriousness of the situation, Lieut.-Col. Seagrim placed himself at the head of his battalion which was, at the time, suffering heavy casualties and led it through the hail of fire. He personally helped the team which was placing the scaling ladder over the anti-tank ditch, and was himself the first to cross it.

"He led the assault, firing his pistol, throwing grenades, and personally assaulting two machine-gun posts which were holding up the advance of one of his companies.

"It is estimated that in this phase he killed or captured twenty Germans. This display of leadership and personal courage led directly to the capture of the objective.

"When dawn broke the battalion was firmly established on the position, which was of obvious importance to the enemy, who immediately made every effort to regain it, and Lieut.-Col. Seagrim was quite undeterred. He moved from post to post organising and directing the fire until the attackers were wiped out to a man.

"By this valour disregard for personal safety and outstanding example he so inspired his men that the battalion successfully took and held its objective, thereby allowing the attack to proceed."

GREEN HOWARDS AT AKARIT

Time-Table of the Advance

IT is exactly 48 days since the attack in Tunisia began. Here is a brief diary of events since then:—

March 20—General Montgomery's attack upon the Mareth Line begins.

March 23—The Eighth Army breaks open Rommel's Mareth positions and begins push to the north.

April 7—The British First Army, after a comparative lull, begins to move and captures El Aouina.

April 4—General Anderson's men take Cape Serrat, and the Eighth Army links up with the Americans.

April 5—The Eighth Army resumes its attack and smashes Rommel's Wadi Akarit line.

April 8—Sfax occupied by the Eighth Army.

April 12—Sousa taken by the Eighth Army. Allied forces in the central sector push on to capture Kairouan.

April 20—Enfidaville falls to General Montgomery.

April 21—Allied general offensive begins along whole front.

April 27—British infantry clear Longstop Hill, north of Medjez el Bah.

May 3—Real threat to Bizerta develops with capture of Mateur by Americans.

May 6—General Allied offensive along whole front. After short lull, Allied offensive continued.

May 7—Tunis and Bizerta captured.

GREEN HOWARDS AT AKARIT

How a Vital Bridgehead was Established

Battalions of the Green Howards played a magnificent part in the Battle of Akarit, the action which resulted in the establishment of a bridgehead in the hills, north of Gabes. British troops had to advance over a bullet-swept plain, where there was very little cover, towards a gap between two lines of hills. Numerous machine-gun nests were concealed in these hills, from which the enemy could enfilade the approaching forces. His artillery was sited so that he could bring down a devastating barrage, and he had established many lines of communicating trenches and a formidable anti-tank ditch.

Major Hull's Story

Major C. Macdonald Hull, M.C., of Edinburgh, describing the part played by a Green Howard battalion, said that its main task was to exploit the bridgehead.

"First light found us just behind the bridgehead," he said, "receiving all the fire the enemy could direct at us. The bridgehead at this time had not definitely been established, so the C.O. decided to get in on the right. This we did; and, before the enemy knew where he was, the leading companies were right in among them. We had taken them completely by surprise by this daylight attack, and the move was very definitely a good one.

"After several sharp exchanges of small-arms fire, the first enemy prisoners were extracted, and then the rot began and they came out in swarms. Sections of our troops attacked on their own; and, although in some cases there was heavy opposition, they went in with their bayonets, rifles and Tommy-guns, and soon overran the enemy. My own company collected between three and four hundred prisoners. We did not escort them, but simply directed them back.

"There were many acts of heroism. One lance-sergeant was fired at by an enemy strong point. With three men he went into the assault with the bayonet and captured the position. He took 60 prisoners despite the fact that they had eight machine-guns.

"A lance-corporal was attacked with his section from two directions. He sent his section to deal with one strong point and tackled the other, single-handed, with his Tommy-gun. He collected 19 prisoners.

"Platoon commanders tackled positions which would normally have necessitated company attacks. We reached our final objective, a point 1,800 yards beyond the anti-tank ditch, and consolidated there. In the evening, the Boche counter-attacked with tanks and infantry; but, with the support of the artillery and machine-gunners from another regiment, we drove them off.

"My sergeant-major passed an enemy weapon pit, not knowing it was there, and after he had done so, the occupants opened fire on him. He turned round and silenced it single-handed."

Major R. J. L. Jackson, of Guisborough, whose duty it was to remain at battalion H.Q., said: "We knew that the forward elements had met with success when we saw the streams of prisoners coming out"; and Sergeant John Clayton, of Hall Farm, Aldborough, Boroughbridge, added that some of the prisoners were laughing and others crying.

This battalion made three big attacks in three weeks—the first on the Mareth outposts, the second on the Mareth Line itself, and the third at Akarit. It is the same battalion that held Gravelines, a vital position in the defence of Dunkirk.

Helped to Save the World from Disaster

50th Division's Proud Record

When the Germans and Italians, flushed with success, were thrusting forward to what they thought would be the easy conquest of Egypt, the 50th (Northumbrian) Division was among the few tired formations who, late in June, 1942, barred the way to the Nile at Alamein and saved the world from disaster.

Throughout the summer of that year they fought through each phase of the North African war, playing a leading part in most of its major events. For the men and women of North-Eastern England, Gazala, Mersa Matruh, El Alamein, Wadi Akarit, Mareth and Enfidaville have become shrines dedicated to the courage and endurance of Northumbria.

The 50th gave an early taste of their high quality in a dashing local action at Fort Capuzzo, which they stormed and held grimly until, their mission accomplished, they withdrew in good order.

At Gazala, when Rommel launched his last offensive and the fortunes of battle elsewhere had made a general retreat necessary, the 50th covered the withdrawal of the South Africans to Tobruk. Then, to save themselves, they struck westward deep into enemy territory, broke through the Axis lines and, swinging south and east, fought for 30 miles before rejoining the Eighth Army on the Egyptian border.

Determined Fighters

Later the 50th held Mersa Matruh for several days; and in each phase of the struggle at Alamein enhanced their reputation as dashing and determined fighters.

They played their part in the Tunisian climax. In the assault of the Mareth Line, they crossed and sealed the deep anti-tank ditch and, with the bayonet, stormed and captured strong points in an elaborate defence system.

At the Wadi Akarit, the 50th went forward into the centre of the Eighth Army's attack. They forced their way across another great anti-tank ditch and held and extended a bridgehead deep in the enemy position, which then became untenable.

Finally, at Enfidaville, the seaward end of the German line fell to them.

British troops in Sicily enjoying a bathe and also a chance to wash their clothes during a brief halt at a mountain stream North of Syracuse.

4: THE WAR YEARS – SICILY AND ITALY

AFTER NORTH AFRICA GEORGE WENT with his unit to Sicily. After landing there, as they advanced there was a small hamlet on a hill. He said he thought "Well, if we go up on the hill we'll see if the Jerries are in there. We didn't know. I thought, 'Well, even if they're not, we'll be in a position where we can see what's going on.' So we clambered up there into this little place. These were funny little houses with two stories. Underneath, the cows and other animals, and then upstairs was where the people lived. And of course they all came out to have a look at us, and they were standing looking at us, and we were looking at them. And I had a Scotsman, one Scotsman in the company. All of a sudden he pointed up to a window and he said, 'Pietro. Come doon here now' So Pietro came doon here now and it turned out he had sold ice cream in Glasgow. That's how this fellow knew him. So I said to him, 'Well, look. You can tell these people we're not here to be a nuisance to them. As long as they're not a nuisance to us, then we aren't interested in them. We're here to drive Mussolini out of Sicily. That's our job. Not to interfere with citizens who behave themselves.' And I think he told them all this and they got very happy and brought out some terrible wine and we all had wine for a bit and then we went on. Eventually, of course, some time later, we did get into fighting. We had a good old scrap all the way right almost up to the end of Sicily. We had some very nasty battles there, but we got on".

After Sicily the army moved on to invade Italy. George said he finally went back to being second in command of a company. He said they came to a big river which they had to cross. The Germans were on the other side. George said "We put in this night attack. We were all bitten by mosquitoes as well as all the other rest of the trouble. A lot of the company got malaria, including my company commander. So I became the company commander. And I became the company commander for the rest of that session, right until we left to come back to England. So we had some exciting times there, yes indeed."

"One day, when we were going along we came to a little village and we thought we'd better have a look in the houses. We surprised two, they must have been sort of Dad's Army people, I think, in uniform. Unfortunately, there they were. They were in uniform. What were we going to do? I think one of them could speak a bit of French. I said, 'Well, what do you do for a living?' One was a hairdresser and the other one was a cook. I said, 'Well, look. There are two things. Either you go back to the prison camp or, if you like, we could do with a barber and a cook. You can come along with us. Have you any money?' They said yes, and they gave me all their money. They thought they were bribing me, but I gave the money to their wives, who were very chuffed. I said to these women, 'We'll look after them' and they joined us."

In a very short time they were dressed in Green Howards uniforms, almost before they knew what had happened. They were very, very popular and the other soldiers were giving them bits of money to buy things. I got a terrific shock once, though, when we put an attack in. There I was lying there and these bullets were flying all over the place. Suddenly one of them came up to me in the front line dragging ammunition. I said 'Get away! They'll shoot you if they get you!' Then the end of the war in Italy came and we were coming back to the UK. My two friends, the two Italians, they were very unchuffed. They thought they were going to come back with us and form part of the British army. There's lots of funny things go on. I don't talk about the bad bits. However, there are terrible casualties and wounded. I shall never forget the most terrible sight that I saw was of a tank with half a man standing up and a solid shot must have cut him in two. The top half of him was lying on the ground. Now, that kind of thing you don't like to keep in your memory very much, do you?"

From Italy George returned to the UK with his Company and the rest of the Battalion to prepare for the invasion.

WE WILL DRIVE THE GERMANS FROM SICILY

GREEN HOWARDS IN ITALY

Among the First Troops to Land

It was officially stated yesterday that the Green Howards have been in action in Italy. They were among the first troops to land there. The formation to which they belong was in action on the Biferno River, and, on October 14, took Casa Calenda and Morrone.

On November 9, it forced a crossing of the River Vandra and captured Forli, on the important road from Isernia to Castel di Sangro. Since then, it has been engaged in the difficult operations in the mountainous centre of the Italian front, where it has seen much hard fighting.

From Our Special Correspondent
J. ILLINGWORTH

The Green Howards, when I was in Italy in October, occupied an advanced position in the hills between Campobasso and Casacalenda, facing the river Biferno, to which one of their patrols, led by Captain "Ted" Roberts, of Farsley, near Leeds, had penetrated on the afternoon that I joined them. The patrol, brilliantly executed, caused the startled Germans occupying two forward machine-gun posts to open fire, without results but betraying their situation, and this information was of considerable value to our troops when they moved forward the following morning.

The Green Howards had just been provided with their winter battledress, of which they were glad; for, though the heavy rain of a day or two before had given way to sunshine, the days were cold in the hills. Their headquarters before they advanced were in a small railway station on a line spanning the hills. Along this line the Germans, in their withdrawal, had blown up the bridges, and our troops were hard at work making diversionary roads, hammering metalling out of great boulders.

"Engineers?" said a watching officer, echoing my question. "Oh, dear, no. These are our own men. There is nothing a Green Howard can't do—or hasn't done since we landed in Sicily."

Extraordinary Marching

They had been among the assault troops at that landing, and had distinguished themselves by some extraordinary marching in full order —"marching," as one of them said, "through the whole of the campaign in Sicily, from beginning to end, faster than the Hun ever thought we could march, and in that way exercising a big influence on the result." They had continued with some hard marching through Italy.

Now they were in this small railway station. The officers' mess was in an upstairs room in the stationmaster's house. From the open window I looked down on the small square where a group of men, in the moonlight, stood round a radio set. A choir somewhere in far-off England were singing some old and lovely hymns, and the sound of their singing filled the square. When the singing stopped in England, it started in the waiting room on this Italian station. These were good Yorkshire voices singing their marching songs. Everyone was in good heart. That night I slept on the floor of the parcels office.

Moving Forward

We moved forward into a morning which was more beautiful than any morning I had known. The mountains lying ahead were swathed in mist; and, rising above the mist, as if floating in the blue air, were the mountain villages.

Once we lay on a bank by the roadside listening to gunfire on our left. Here Captain John Bade, of Middlesbrough, told me how, a day or two before, he had put into an ambulance and sent to hospital a 10-year-old boy who had been injured on a German mine.

"Three hours afterwards," he said, "we were receiving a tremendous deputation from the village. It was headed by the village doctor leading two mules. Slung across the mules were two sacks. The doctor introduced a woman from the crowd as the mother of the boy, and explained that she wished us to take the contents of the two sacks because she was grateful for our treatment of her boy. In the sacks were flour, eggs and chickens."

When I left them, the Green Howards were moving in on the village of Petrella. Some of the men, stripped to the waist, were digging slit trenches against expected mortar fire. All the time there was steady fire on our left, but none came to the Green Howards.

"Give our love to Yorkshire," the men called as I left. They went into Petrella that night without incident. The Germans had gone.

What impressed me about the whole movement was the great care put into its preparation. No hazard was left unprospected.

5: THE WAR YEARS – D-DAY

LATE IN HIS LIFE GEORGE gave at least two substantial interviews about his experience in the D-Day landings and the action that followed. One was given in 2004, published under the heading "The luck of the 'Bolo'" in the Summer 2009 edition of EVERYONE'S WAR – the Journal of The Second World War Experience Centre, and subsequently reprinted in THE GREEN HOWARD and in the 2010 edition of THE COLCESTRIAN. Another was given to Jim Acheson when he recorded an interview with George about his memories. This was produced as a DVD "Memories of Major George 'Bolo' Young MC MA". In what follows I have used the first as the basis, adding some additional material from the DVD.

In George's words "I was Company Commander of B Company and we were preparing to land on Gold Beach. Strange as it may seem, some time before we sailed, one of my platoon commanders had been taken in a submarine from which he swam ashore, had a look at the place we were going to land and returned. From the intelligence reports we knew that there would be a short piece of sand, then a big minefield covered with Dannert wire. Beyond that there was a big anti-tank ditch in the sand and then a ridge. I thought for a bit about this and decided that if they had fixed line fire on the beach they would not believe that anyone would be so stupid as to crawl into a minefield so there would not be those fixed lines of fire on that. I said to my troops 'Whatever happens you must not stop on the beach! Whatever you do you must get up and crawl under the German wire that surrounds the minefield because they won't have their fields of fire doing shooting along there.' And I said 'But once you stop on the beach you won't get up again.'

Eventually we got into the old landing craft and were going along and I was carrying a large jar of rum to issue to people, a great big earthenware thing, and so I offered this around – and nobody wanted any.

"We got up to the shore, and the Naval officer in charge, I think he lost his nerve a bit. He gave the orders for the front to fall down and he said 'There you are, Sir' and saluted me smartly. I ran out into about ten feet of water and the boat went over the top of me. A lot of people were drowned that way – a lot of people. But as luck would have it, it was the old George Young luck. As I went down I must have taken a breath, and I remember clearly that I kicked out with my left boot and hit a large bolt underneath the bottom of the vessel and shot out at the side. Then I was really swimming to shore. Unfortunately I had ripped the sole of the boot.

I think the Naval Officer must have taken the boat in a bit further for the other men. By the time I got to the beach there was nobody on it and nothing happening. The men had all crawled under the German wire and were waiting for the flail tanks which were coming to deal with the mines. I rushed up shouting 'I'm in charge! I'm in charge!'. There was no fire, nobody fired at us, so we got through the line with the help of the flail tanks who flailed a way through for us and we got into the anti-tank ditch which was all sand. We lined up and I said 'Well come on, lads! On we go!' and ran up with the Sergeant Major and got out.

The men were carrying 120 rounds of ammunition, and the weight of all they had to carry was too much, so as they ran up they slipped back again. So we stopped running and found ourselves walking towards the enemy without any support, as if we were on a Sunday afternoon stroll. My Sergeant Major said 'What are we going to do?'. I said 'Well let's walk until they start firing'. So we walked on and by this time the men behind us were starting to scramble out a bit and we walked right up to the enemy's front line. These Germans they were staring at us. Incredible, isn't it?

I think their officers had been called away to a meeting and there was nobody there to give them any instructions. I had a packet of fifty cigarettes in my pocket and luckily it hadn't suffered in the water because it was covered with cellophane. So I took it out, chucked the cigarettes down at them and pointed back to the shore. We took 120 prisoners without a shot being fired."

(N.B. Jean-Pierre Dupont, Curator of the Gold Beach Museum, had been 10 years old at the time of the landings. His family's house was close to where George landed. It was mentioned in air reconnaissance reports at the time as the "lavatory pan house" because of its shape when seen from above. His parents had taken the family to stay in Paris a few days before D-Day, so he was not there at the time. However, he said that the troops who surrendered to George were not Germans but men who had been captured by them on the Eastern front and forced to fight for them. That perhaps helps to explain why, in the absence of their officers, they did not open fire.)

"We continued over the meadows until we came to this little village of Crépon, and I rang up the Commanding officer and told him there were some Germans there. He said 'Stay there. We will join you' and so the Battalion arrived and D Company attacked the village. That was where the famous VC was won by Stan Hollis.

We went on scrapping away for a bit and we had to be brought back because we were too far forward. One of the strange things about military tactics is that I think the higher you are in rank, the more you like to see a straight line, which is of course quite absurd because nature has no straight lines, so when you are on the ground you really have to be there to see what to do, and this I think was the cause of our downfall later on.

We had a very odd Brigadier. He summoned us all and gave us a talk. My Battalion Commander, Colonel Hastings, was sitting behind him among all the other senior officers. This chap gave us a great talk and then he said 'Remember, gentlemen, no prisoners will be taken!' A look of Bolo must have come over my face because Colonel Hastings, behind him, pointed first to his lips and then to the side of his head. So I shut up." (As George later pointed out, it was obvious to any one who thought about it that when the Germans realised that they would not be taken prisoner if they surrendered, they would fight to the death.)

"It was this Brigadier who sent us into battle in a most remarkably stupid way. We had advanced through the village of Ducy-Sainte- Marguerite and other delightfully named villages and were on the end of a meadow. We saw that there was a bit of the Bocage, a bit of woodland, on a high point ahead of us. The Brigadier sent one tank up to have a look. This tank went up during the morning and reported back that there were no Germans there. They can't have been very efficient. Based on what happened later I doubt whether they really looked anywhere. I bet they were a bit windy and just went up and came back.

So the Brigadier said 'Well there's nobody there. Go up and occupy it.' I went with the leading company to occupy it. As we got through a cornfield and came out onto a flat bit, everything opened up. There was a Panzer Division there. Those bloody stupid people in the tank can't even have gone round the back of the little wood on the top to see what was there. What's more, the Brigadier didn't send another couple of tanks up to cover us as we advanced. That was incredible. We came under a tremendous blistering lot of fire. In addition there were snipers up in the trees. We were really caught and had to go to ground.

My company was very badly knocked about. One of the soldiers not far from me was wounded and I crawled out and brought him back into the Company Headquarters and stood up to get my first field dressing out of my pocket. At that moment an 88 millimetre exploded behind me. A large fragment went through the edge of my arm and went into my back and I hit the deck.

Almost immediately, my old friend Major Honeyman, who was in charge of A Company, went through to continue the attack as I lay there. He said 'Oh, hello, Bolo'. I was lying there flat on my stomach with my face turned round to the side. I thought to myself 'Funny. You're going to your death. I think we're going to lose you.' As he passed me the Sergeant Major, who remembered me from when I was in A Company said 'Your motto, sir, you can't whack a bit of active service'.

I lay there and as luck would have it, after a short time, Sergeant-Major Hollis, who won the VC, came past and saw me there. He commandeered a tank retiring from the line and sent it back. It stopped and a chap put his head out of the tank and, seeing people standing around, said 'What have you got there then?' My men replied 'We have the Company Commander. He's badly wounded'. He said 'What kind of an old bugger is he?' They said 'He's alright, he's alright, one of the best.' He said 'Well, get him up on the front and I'll hold him on.' And he got out of his tank, held me on in the front and we went through with the shells still bursting and fire all over the place. What a brave man – I could never discover who exactly he was – who risked his life. But that's a good soldier, isn't it? I was conscious all the time. I am one of the luckiest persons alive aren't I? I was never in real pain.

The tank took me back through these great hedgerows until we got back to a first field dressing place. They put me in a corner on the stretcher while they were chopping away, all the surgeons, in this place. They were operating and operating on people and I lay there. After quite a long time, one of them came over and said 'How are you?' I said 'Well, alright I suppose. I might be worse. I could do with a cup of tea.' He said 'You couldn't drink a cup of tea. What happened?'

I said 'Well, first of all, I've got a wound here on my arm. It's lucky it happened to me there and whatever it was went through there, but I've still got full articulation with my fingers.' He said 'Are you a doctor then?' I said 'No, just educated.' He said 'I'm not going to touch you. No, I'm not going to touch you. We must get you down to the shore to the next place.'

They took me down to the beach where there was a large hospital tent. They put me on a bed there and the next morning the padre arrived to ask me if I wanted the last rites. I said 'Well I hadn't really thought about it, but I don't think I'll bother for a bit, if you don't mind.' He went away and came back with the medical officer. He said 'I don't know what we are going to do with you.' I said 'Well, can you find me something to read? I can't lie here all day.' He said You're too ill for that. You couldn't read anything.' I said 'Try me.' They went away and came back with an illustrated magazine and gave it to me. I opened it. They were dead right, I couldn't see anything, except that there was obviously a funny cartoon in the middle of the page. Summoning up all my brilliance, I said 'Look at that, Doc. That's jolly good, isn't it?' He looked at it and then looked at me and said 'Well, yes. We must get you to the shore for the hospital ship.'

They got me down to the shore. I was in another tent and the next morning I was taken down to the water's edge. A large number of civilians with little boats had come over to help. One of these chaps put me on a stretcher across his little motorboat, with the ends over the sides of the boat. We found a hospital ship and they hoisted me aboard by sending down four hooks, which went on the corners of the stretcher.

I landed on the deck and a young nurse came and looked at me. She said 'How are you, son?' I replied 'I'm alright, Grandma.' Then they came to take a photograph of me. They were going to take an x-ray. I said to them when they got my clothes off 'If you stuck a rose in my mouth you could take a photograph of this. It would get a lot of money back home.'

They didn't want to operate on me on the ship. Nobody would touch the wound. So we went all the way back to Southampton. There I was taken to the hospital and put in a bed there. There the 'Bolo' luck continued. It so happened that a famous surgeon had come down from St. Bartholomew's Hospital to operate on an Admiral. When he discovered that I was there and among the first of the casualties arriving, he said he would operate on me. He did.

The next morning when he saw me, he said 'My word, you were lucky. A y-shaped piece of shrapnel had gone right through your back and come to rest touching your aorta. And when I say touching, when I took it away there was a mark there where it was pressing against your aorta. if it had gone only another millimetre you'd have been dead in five minutes.' So, although it was the end of my fighting career, I bore a charmed life. I was lucky. Always lucky."

The award of the Military Cross

After George had described this experience on D-Day and the fighting that followed, Jim said "You have not mentioned your MC." George replied "Actually there's another story there, you see. It's story after story. Patterson was a private soldier in my company, and when we came back to England before D-Day we went up to this place near Garboldisham in Norfolk, and the villagers there were very kind. We had a day off and they heard we were having this day off and said 'Well there's nowhere for them to go, nothing much to do here, we'll give them a lunch.' So I summoned the company the night before and said 'There'll only be one parade tomorrow and that will be at 8 o'clock.' I didn't tell them about the lunch. I thought I would surprise them. At roll call Patterson was absent. All the rest of them went and had their lunch. Then Patterson came back. So he was marched in to me for being absent. And I said 'Well you're a silly chap, aren't you? If you had stayed you would have had a lunch, but now you're up for trouble for being absent without leave. The least I can do is to give you seven days confined to billets.' He replied 'I'm not going to do it.' I said 'Sergeant Major, I didn't quite catch what he said. Would you take him out and explain to him that this is a serious business.' So the Sergeant Major took him out and brought him back in again. I said 'Now then, I will say to you seven days CB.' He said 'I'm not going to do it.' I said 'Patterson, if I had heard that, you would have to be court marshalled. And it would have been a very serious business, and you would have paid a lot for this. So, let me tell you that if you say I'm dealing with you unfairly, you have a right to go before the Commanding Officer of the battalion.' 'Well' he said, 'I'll do that.' So I said 'Very good. See that he's up with Orders this afternoon.'

So at Orders time I went up there and there's old Patterson there. The Regimental Sergeant Major came up to me and said 'Private Patterson would like a word with you, sir.' So I went over to him and said 'What is it, Patterson?' 'The lads tell me that you've got me bang to rights, sir' he said, 'I realize that, can I withdraw?' And I said 'Yes, if you do the seven days CB.' He said 'Yes, sir.' So he did the seven days CB, and I sent for him and said 'Well, you know, you're a funny chap but you've got some guts. I mean you tried to stand up to me, and you were almost trying to stand up to the Commanding Officer. But why don't you come in on our side, and let me make you a Lance Corporal?' And he looked at me and said 'Well, yes sir.'

So he became a Lance Corporal, and on the day I was wounded he forced his way up to the presence of the Commanding Officer, Colonel Hastings, and refused to go away until they had told him that they were going to put me in for a MC, because I had behaved in such a way that all the other soldiers admired what I'd done for them. So I was given the medal not from an officer, but from a Lance Corporal. That's how I got my MC, but I don't think I did much more that day than others, but still there you are"

Addendum

For many years after the war George visited Normandy to commemorate the D-Day landings. In 2004, on the occasion of the 60th anniversary, at the age of 93 he was the highest ranking surviving officer from the 6th Battalion the Green Howards. As such he was invited to accept the salute from surviving members of the battalion at a ceremony held at Crepon, close to where he won his Military Cross. In this year, as in other years when celebrating with other veterans the liberation of the village of Crepon, he was the welcome guest of a Normandy family. In addition, on 4th of June 2006 he took part in a ceremony to unveil the Hollis VC Hut at Vers-sur-Mer. He also gave his uniform to the Gold Beach Museum there where it is exhibited, along with his medals which his daughter, Alison, donated in 2018.

Ilkley Officer Wounded

News has been received that Major G. M. Young (33), Hillside, Middleton, Ilkley, was brought to this country from France last week suffering from wounds in the abdomen and in the arm. For three months, after joining the Army in 1940, Major Young was with the Scots Guards; after that he was transferred to another unit with a commission, and fought with that regiment in North Africa and Sicily last year. Before the war, he held the post of second English master at Blackpool Grammar School. In 1938 Major Young married Miss E. A. Stavert, daughter of Mrs. and the late Canon Stavert, of Hillside, Middleton.

Press announcement of his injury kept by his wife, Eve.

C.S.M. Hollis—a Man Without Fear

From JOE ILLINGWORTH,
"Yorkshire Post" War Correspondent

NORMANDY, Thursday Night

This is the story of Company Sergt.-Major Stanley Hollis, aged 29, of Farnville North, Old Ormesby, Middlesbrough, who has won the Victoria Cross while serving with D Company of a battalion of the Green Howards.

He was described to me by the Commanding Officer of his company, Major Ronald Lofthouse, of Newcastle, as "a man who seems to be absolutely without fear." Major Lofthouse added: "On at least three occasions in the Normandy fighting he performed V.C. deeds. He has in fact a whole chapter of gallant acts to his name. In every attack we have made he has done something outstanding. He is absolutely brilliant."

C.S.M. Hollis stands over 6ft., is "broadly and beautifully built," and has a quick eye. It was his quick eye, as well as his fearlessness, which won him the V.C.

It was he who first saw the tip of the Spandau slowly and cautiously appearing in the slit of an apparently empty pillbox just behind the beaches on D-Day. He stormed the pillbox with grenade and Sten gun. It was he who, some distance away down what seemed to be a deserted lane, saw two dogs with their backs towards him wagging their tails.

Dogs Wagged Their Tails

C.S.M. Hollis wanted to know why they were wagging their tails. With Major Lofthouse he crept down the lane. They came to the corner of a farmhouse round which the dogs had disappeared, and round the corner they saw a German field gun and its crew. The Green Howards attacked the gun, its crew lowered it and began to fire at them at point blank range.

C.S.M. Hollis crawled into the open with a Bren gun, exposing himself to heavy fire, and covered his company while they withdrew. He has since been wounded and evacuated to England.

The commanding officer of his battalion has sent him the following message:—

"All ranks of the battalion send their heartiest congratulations and deeply appreciate the great honour which your award has brought to your regiment."

This message was flown to England by the American Air Force. The full story of C.S.M. Hollis since he landed on the beach on D-Day has been told to me by Major Lofthouse.

His company's job was to capture a four-gun coastal battery at Mont Fleury. They waded 100 yards to the shore through a rough sea and under mortar fire, and slipped through a minefield towards a big white house which was their landmark. The command post for the battery was about 100 yards to the right of the house. The battery lay some distance behind the command post. One platoon captured the house without a great deal of trouble. The two other platoons prepared to attack the battery.

Missed at 15 Yards

C.S.M. Hollis, who was commanding a two-inch mortar group, was laying down smoke across the front of the battery. But he was keeping his sharp eye open all the time. He noticed that the troops who were going in to attack the battery were bypassing the command post. He called Major Lofthouse's attention to this and the two of them went over and investigated the post. It was made up of two concrete pill boxes. They found the first of these empty.

"What happened after that was one hell of a scramble," said Major Lofthouse. "As I came back round the empty pill box I saw" C.S.M. Hollis run to the second pill box 20 or 30 yards away. He was running hell for leather for it and firing his Sten gun from the hip as he ran. I then saw that there was a Spandau sticking out of the slit in the pill box. The Spandau fired two bursts at him at 15 yards range. They missed him—it was a complete miracle that they did.

"Split-second Affair"

"I saw him clear past 15 yards and jump on to the pill box. I saw him put another magazine in his Sten gun. Then he leaned over the other side, flung a grenade into the pill box and then went in, emptying his magazine as he disappeared.

"When he came out he had five or six prisoners in front of him. He had left two dead Germans in the pill box." It was a remarkable act. I saw that pill box afterwards. It was a real West Wall pill box, an affair of massive concrete. Only one foot of it showed above ground, but below there were two Spandau to it.

He captured this with its radio and telephones all intact, and he prevented the company—which was making the attack on the gun battery—from being fired on from behind. He told me he had seen the Spandau appearing in the slit of the pill box and that after that he had acted instinctively. It was a split-second affair.

The Green Howards went on and stormed the gun battery, taking a large number of prisoners. They moved on to Crepon. In Crepon C.S.M. Hollis hurried up to Major Lofthouse and suggested they should investigate a back lane which they had just passed. He said that he had seen two dogs wagging their tails at the end of the lane. The lane and its neighbourhood looked deserted, but if it was deserted why were the two dogs wagging their tails?

Attack on Field Gun

The two went cautiously up the lane, and round the corner of a farm house they saw a German field gun and its crew. Major Lofthouse decided to put in a full platoon attack on the gun. While one section opened fire from farm buildings, C.S.M. Hollis took a Bren gun section into the open on the flank. The attack from the farm buildings was unable to make any progress because of the buildings which impeded them.

"The gun crews' defensive elements had mounted their machine-guns and were giving us stick," said Major Lofthouse. C.S.M. Hollis realised that something had gone wrong, and though under heavy fire he crawled round so as to find out why.

"When he saw what was happening he got hold of a two-inch mortar and crawled to a gap in the wall. He was under direct fire there, but it was the only point from which he could see explosive on the battery.

"The attack, however, could still make no progress. The gun could not get over the wall. They were knocked down as soon as they got on top of it. C.S.M. Hollis got hold of a Piat gun and was about to fire it when the barrel of the field gun was lowered and began to fire at us over open sites. We were only 100 yards from the gun. It was point blank range.

"The gun struck the farm buildings immediately behind us and masonry was flung over us from all directions. The gun was firing twelve rounds to the minute."

The company decided to bypass the gun position and take it from the rear. But the movement of the enemy fire was now being directed on the Bren group, and they could not get out. Major Lofthouse decided to put in another Bren group to cover their withdrawal. C.S.M. Hollis at once volunteered to take out his second group. This he did. He himself took a Bren gun and crawled into a completely exposed position.

Hit by Sniper

"He has a lot of difficulty in getting there," said Major Lofthouse. "He was under fire. A sniper shot at him and the bullet cut a tiny furrow across his forehead but did not knock him out. He was in frightful danger, but he was also in a good forward position and under his hot covering fire the other Bren gunners were able to crawl back and out of range.

"When they had all got away he crawled out himself, still under fire, and rejoined the platoon."

The company abandoned its attack on the gun, under orders to push further into Normandy.

That is what C.S.M. Hollis did on D-Day. His brave story has continued since.

An N.C.O. was shot by a sniper, and the Company Sergeant-Major volunteered to go out and bring him back," said Major Lofthouse. "We sent out a Bren-gun carrier with a Vickers machine-gun mounted on it. The Sergeant-Major walked alongside it for 500 yards, not knowing when he was going to bump into the sniper. He walked into an open cornfield where the corn was breast high and searched through it. He found the N.C.O., but he was dead. He picked him up and brought him in. There was a big rope about 200 yards from the cornfield, and when we cleared it later with a couple of tanks we found ten Boches who had been sitting there while he searched the cornfield."

C.S.M. Hollis crawled down the bank, flung in a grenade and then dashed 15 yards across the open to the farm building. He found that his grenade had knocked the Spandau crew out. As he turned he saw a German levelling his rifle from a slit trench. He rushed him and killed him with his Sten gun.

"Almost a Legend"

"On another occasion we were reorganising after an attack. We were in a very sticky position," said Major Lofthouse. "We had no slit trenches. While we were reorganising C.S.M. Hollis saw a Browning gun mounted on one of our knocked out tanks, and he climbed up and took it off. He thought it would be useful. It was. He had no sooner got it down than he saw three Germans crawling up to our positions.

"They were within 100 yards of our forward troops. Mortar fire was coming down, but in spite of this he rushed off along a sunken track, got the Browning in position, fired off a complete belt and killed all three of the enemy. This saved the situation for us," said Major Lofthouse. He added: "He did all kinds of other deeds which do not read as sensationally as these in every minute of every attack. He is almost a legend in the battalion. The men would do anything for him. He really has been a first rate sergeant-major."

Major Lofthouse said that C.S.M. Hollis was wounded during a night attack in Sicily. "But he came back in double-quick time for more action. He was one of the high lights of the sergeants' mess. He was a singer of hill billy songs."

Contemporary press report of CSM Hollis VC

Major George 'Bolo' Young, commander B Company of 6th Battalion, The Green Howards (Alexandra, Princess of Wales' Own Yorkshire Regiment), was 33 when he came ashore on GOLD BEACH King on the 6th of June 1944. He was a battle hardened veteran who fought with the 8 Army during the North African campaign and took part in the amphibious landings in Sicily in July 1943. He was wounded at Cristot, five days after the landing and awarded the MC for bravery.

Major George Young MC, in 2007, presented his Officer's Service Dress uniform to the GOLD BEACH Museum who have decided to have it on display as a token of gratitude to the Green Howards who fought in Normandy and particularly an act of remembrance to those of the regiment who fell for the liberation of Europe.

These medals, reproductions of those won by Major Young, were donated and mounted by Graham Cufley, a member of the Gold Beach Living History Group, in February 2008.

Previous page and above: The model of George in his uniform and the accompanying description are in the Gold Beach Museum at Vers-sur-Mer. In 2018 George's daughter, Alison, presented the actual medals to the museum.

Jean-Pierre Dupont, the Curator of the Gold Beach Museum, showing the Sharp family some of the exhibits on their visit to Normandy in 2016. The picture of George and his medals can be seen in the background.

A tribute to George in a café in Bayeux.

6: COLCHESTER ROYAL GRAMMAR SCHOOL

THE WOUND ENDED GEORGE'S ACTIVE service and he was confined to a non-combatant role for the remainder of his military service. After demobilisation he returned to his teaching post at Blackpool Grammar School.

In 1947 he applied for a post teaching English at CRGS. In his own words "Called for an interview with Mr. Fletcher during the 1947 summer holidays at a now defunct hotel in Saffron Walden, I was welcomed by a burly smiling man, whose first question was 'Would you like a drink? I thanked him, and luckily, before I had time to suggest anything alcoholic, he said 'Tea or Coffee?'

"Some days later he wrote and offered me the job. The arrival of his letter coincided with an issue of the Times Educational Supplement, advertising the vacancy of the Headmastership of CRGS. The combination of events led my colleagues at Blackpool Grammar School to suggest that, overcome with remorse at having engaged me to replace a certain Mr. Ormandy, he had promptly handed in his resignation and fled to one of the more remote colonies.

"But there he was, in the Headmaster's House, when I called in just before Christmas and we had a fascinating conversation about taking blackcurrant cuttings, after which he advised me to contact the Second Master, who was to be in charge until a new Headmaster was found. Consequently I went round to Wellesley Road and made the acquaintance of Mr. and Mrs. F. W. Seymour. Fred, as I later learned to call him, who deserves full credit for his service to the school, gave me a great welcome, as did 'Mammy', and their kindness put me at my ease."

Writing in 1984, George said that by lunch time on his first day in January 1948 he had made the acquaintance of many boys and members of staff, who were to become firm friends. On that first day, in the period before lunch, David Donaldson recollects him "striding zestfully – almost, one might say, erupting – into Upper V's classroom off the School Hall. Having reached his desk, he turned to face us, a tall, spare, moustachioed figure and barked 'My name is Young, George Young. I'm 38 years old and I was a Major in the army. I got the MC for capturing a German jam factory. Now to poetry and Sorearse and Rustibum to you, but Sohrab and Rustum to the examiners!'" (The mention of "capturing a German jam factory" was clearly George's joke to make an impression. His explanation of the real reason he received the MC is given at the end of the last chapter.)

David added that it was hardly surprising that some lines of that poem were still imprinted on his memory more than 50 years later. He also said that by the end of that inspiring first lesson from George he "presumed to ask him to become attached to School House (shortly afterwards to be renamed Shaw-Jeffrey's

House). He agreed, and it was to prove an attachment greatly to the benefit of all members of the House, and myself in particular, for my remaining years at CRGS."

At the end of that period, the last before lunch, George said he met Casey or "The Baron", as he was known to all students. "'You'd better come and have lunch with us', he said. And so we went off to the lunch hut, and I said 'I don't think I want to sit on the staff table. I think I'll go and sit on a table with some of the students.' He said 'What on earth for?' I said 'Well, I think I want to get to know them.' He said 'Get to know them?' However George did go and sit on a table with some of those from Upper V whom he had just been teaching. (He said he sat next to me, although I must confess that his memory was much better than mine – Alan Sharp).

This brief incident illustrates an important part of George's approach to the job of teaching. Asked by Jim Acheson what makes a good teacher, George replied "Well, the first thing is you really want to do the job. You're not doing it for the salary. You're doing it to teach people, to inculcate something into them which will be some use to them in their lives. You're a servant in a way, aren't you? They don't realize this. You're trying to get them to make something of themselves. You've got to get to know them because you've got to get to know their difficulties as they've got them. Mind you, you can never do quite enough because it's rather difficult to get information without appearing to be interfering. But you get to know something, like their father hasn't got much of a job or so and so. So you know some of them have got problems and some of them haven't, and you can help them, can't you. And they all knew they could come and talk to me, didn't they?

"I haven't mentioned the student part of the Grammar School quite as I should have done. They were all, or nearly all of them, pretty sensible people. They were there because they had ability. Otherwise they wouldn't have passed the 11+, you know. Although many of them came from what I call, and I don't mean it rudely, humble homes. They had parents who perhaps hadn't received much of an education themselves, but were very pleased that their sons could come to the Grammar School. Most of the parents helped and encouraged them. They formed a pretty good band of boys. What with being up on the field playing games with them, and teaching them and doing the plays, you got very close to them and you found them a delightful family to live amongst. That was my reward – and it was a great reward. My reward was when the pupils were happy and learning, and working, because I thought those were the three things you had to do. You had to work hard, you had to learn and, if you were lucky, you could be happy."

George taught English at CRGS from 1948 to 1965. In that time it can be said that this was but one aspect of his massive contribution to the life of the School and of the students. David Donaldson was quoted earlier, commenting how securing George's attachment to School House, shortly afterwards renamed Shaw Jeffrey's House, had proved of great benefit to all its members. While he was not Housemaster, his encouragement and enthusiastic support for members' efforts on the sports field contributed in no small measure to their success. There he was regularly to be heard shouting 'Come on Shaw Jeffreys' or 'Well played, Shaw Jeffreys'. George felt the house system was important. In the 1950s, as he noted, "The House competitions, eagerly contested at all levels, gave most of the boys an opportunity to play for a regular team, if only on a few occasions, and many of the participants of the humbler echelons improved enough to continue playing for many years after they left school." Writing in 1984 he said "Today, of course, the academic standing of the school could hardly be higher and success in sport, both in team games and individual skill, is evident at the highest level. But I cannot help thinking of those early Fifties when the Singer Cup was so fiercely sought after that more than a hundred boys and other spectators came to see School House beat Parrs and win the Senior Rugby Knock-Outs."

George also took on the task of running the school Under 14 Cricket and Rugby teams. In the early 1940s the only junior teams were at Under 15 level and known as the Colts. From his very first year in 1948 George ran Under 14 Cricket and Rugby teams. To encourage members and to promote the teams he even produced an Under 14 magazine, carrying reports of matches. The next year this became "THE COLT". In the June 1949 edition No. 1 George's editorial stated

"The apparent success of last year's Under 14 magazine led us to suppose that there was a future for an enlarged version and here is the first number. It has been delayed by a series of events, but, we hope, is welcome better late than never. We have joined forces with the Under 15 now, and have therefore chosen a title more pertinent to our new function. The style is meant to be vivacious rather than academic, the intention is to amuse as well as instruct, and forgiveness is requested in advance for the manifold mistakes and poor printing. The chief fault, we would like to think, lies in the quality of the type in our old typewriter."

This edition opens with an article by I.D.Prior on Wicket-Keeping. Ian Prior was then 1st XI Captain. Later he was to play for Suffolk and in sides representing the Minor Counties against the touring sides, including the West Indies. This article was followed by a number of reports of matches played. The following reports give a flavour of George's style which as he said in his editorial was "meant to be vivacious rather than academic" and intended "to amuse as well as instruct".

TODDLER'S FIELD-DAY

Or

FROST'S BENEFIT.

Endsleigh won the toss and put the school in to bat. Last week's order, then occasioned by the exhausted condition of Leatherdale, was adhered to, and Palmer and Frost faced the opening overs of Parker and Maskery. Parker bowled round the wicket and made the ball move over quite appreciably to the off, while Maskery maintained a fairly steady length which attracted complete attention and respect of both batsmen.

SLOW BUT SURE

Runs came slowly at the meagre rate of one an over until Parker sent some down wide of the left-handed Frost's legs and these were despatched rather perfunctorily. At the other end Palmer seemed to be mastering the flighted deliveries of Maskery who gave way to Knott, another right arm round bowler. His third ball rapped Palmer's pads, he appealed and the scoreboard read :- 23-1-8. Herbert played quite nicely until the score had mounted to 37 of which he had made only two to Frost's twenty. Stone now displaced Parker. Frost hit the second ball for three and Herbert chopped the next but one on to his wicket in a Palmerian manner:- 40-2-2. Wright now came in at an awkward juncture; more runs were obviously needed and the rate of scoring had now reached three an over. He played very steadily and Frost seemed to quieten down as well. Still the score crept up and Maskery and Parker returned to an attack but it was quite clear that the sting had gone out of the bowling. About ten minutes later both batsmen decided to press the pace. Frost completed a well deserved and well applauded 50. Wright now gave a catch gratefully accepted by square-leg; the scoreboard read 82-3-12. Evans came in running as in a 440 yards and once more the show was on. Being left-handed he appreciated Parker's going away ball and clouted it smartly away for four but was L.B.W. to the next. Captain Richardson scored a nimble five not out and, no doubt with his eyes on the averages, declared at 93-4-4.

Stone and Ashcroft opened the batting and Wright started from the Pavilion end with an innocuous one followed by a succession of curate's egg like deliveries which matched those of Leatherdale at the other end until the eighth over arrived with quiet pomp. Leatherdale then clean bowled Ashcroft :- 6-1-0.

WRIGHT TURNS ON THE HEAT

Next to go was the diminutive but gallant Stone who had collected seven runs. He was completely defeated by a fast delivery from Wright which would have knocked the bat out of his hands if he had put it in the way. Wright now proceeded to bowl faster and more accurately than before and bore all before him like some vast sirocco or khamsoon. His final analysis read 8 for 8. Leatherdale, who took two for nothing, dismissed the wily and dangerous Parker who gave a catch behind the wicket. All out 13 of which five were byes!

(John Wright or "Toddler", as he was commonly called, later became a very successful batsman for Colchester and East Essex C.C., which he captained, and for Essex County C.C. 2nd XI. He also played four times for the county, three times in the County Championship and once against the Pakistan tourists.)

THE UNDER FIFTEEN COLTS XI v WESTCLIFF

Another colourful opening was staged for us in this game. Before Evans had a chance to face a delivery his partner called very late for a run. Evans, like Ado Annie, couldn't say no, and there he was, a flurry of arms and legs and head and bat, half way across the pitch when his wicket was struck down most cruelly. This event had a leavening effect and Patterson and Wheeler batted very soberly if a little uneasily at times. They both fluttered their bats dangerously at deliveries on the off-side of the wicket – a spectacle which pleases a bowler's heart. The unfortunate thing about Wheeler's batting is that it seems as though he is firmly convinced that there are only two wickets behind him, the middle and the leg. In this match, as always, he had a perfectly good off-stump as off-stumps go, and as off-stumps go his went. This was at 17. Two runs later Patterson suddenly decided that now was the time to begin to make merry. He stepped across his wicket and endeavoured to hook to leg a straight good length ball. The stroke was of academic interest only and bore no relation whatsoever to the incidence or flight of the ball. The rest of the team then, in various ways, delivered themselves up severally to the enemy. All except for Ransom and Downing who put on a last wicket partnership of 23 invaluable runs to bring the score up to a very modest 56 runs.

There was a commendable appearance about our bowling that day and it was refreshing to note that anyone who bowled consistently short of a length was replaced immediately. Patterson took 2 for 9, Rolfe 2 for 7 and Westwood had a field day with 6 for 14 runs. Westwood's bowling was a thing of curves and spin and gentle persuasion. He is not one for torturing his victims; they soon realise that they are not for this world when they face his deliveries, and they die quickly, quietly and goodnaturedly.

We eventually won the match by 13 runs, but it was a sketchy victory without much substance to it.

We hope for better things as the season progresses.

George's encouragement did much to enthuse members, both on the Cricket and Rugby fields, leading to their personal enjoyment and to individual and team success. It also led to the production of a steady flow of skilful performers for the more senior teams.

Apart from his contribution in the classroom and on the sports fields, he put on the School Play every year, producing and directing a stream of very successful dramatic productions. When interviewing George, Jim Acheson remarked that his first Shakespeare play was George's production of Julius Caesar and he still remembered it, well over 30 years later. George said "That wasn't a bad performance, was it? We did some jolly good ones, didn't we? I think this was a marvellous thing for you to see these plays and be in them and get to know what the theatre is about, even if only in a small way." Asked what was his favourite performance of all those he did at the school, he replied "Well we did a very good performance of 'The Strong and the Lonely'. That was very good, wasn't it? I can still see Allen Martin sitting in the chair, and tapping with his finger when the chap was getting a bit boring. He was very good. And Tim Hughes, he was very good, too."

David Forder, who came to Colchester to take charge of the old Repertory Theatre in Colchester High Street, and subsequently ran the Mercury Theatre, said that George's productions of school plays were legendary. On at least one occasion the local paper suggested that a play must have been directed by somebody from London! Very many years after leaving school, former students still talked of productions with which they had been involved, – the open air production of Henry V, Macbeth, Twelfth Night, Hamlet, Julius Caesar, St. Joan, The Devil's Disciple......They also remembered trips to London to see productions including one of Macbeth on the reconstruction of an Elizabethan stage, The Cherry Orchard, Much Ado About Nothing, Richard III. In addition Paul Carr, who subsequently designed the set for a school production of Hamlet, based on that at the Mermaid Theatre, and Peter Fenning were taken to meet Bernard Miles and hear his advice.

George believed strongly that to be able to teach students you had to get to know them. Hence his comment on his first day at CRGS that he wanted to sit with some of the students at lunch. Apart from his contact in the classroom he also got to know them through his extracurricular work on the playing fields with the house teams and junior cricket and rugby sides, and through the many dramatic productions. In addition, as John Shrimplin pointed out many years later, running the CRGS Book Room gave him contact with every boy in the school. In getting to know boys he learned – and often addressed them by – their nicknames, where they had any. See his reference to "TODDLER'S FIELD DAY" in the extract from "THE COLT" quoted above. Indeed on occasions where they had none he invented them. He got to know those he taught so well that it was said that he never forgot anyone he had ever taught. Certainly many meeting him again many years after leaving school were astonished not only that he knew who they were but at how much he remembered about them. Tim Hughes telephoned George fifty years after leaving school, having had no contact with him in that time. When George answered, Tim said "You won't know who this is, sir." He was astonished when George responded "I would know that voice anywhere, Mothproof!"

In 1965 George left CRGS and joined the staff of Colchester Institute, where initially he taught General Studies. After a year he transferred to teaching English literature and was put in charge of the Greyfriars annex until his retirement in 1973. However he retained very strong links with the school and with former students for the rest of his life. He joined the Old Colcestrian Society early in his time at the School and regularly attended Society events. He ran Old Time Music Halls to raise funds for the school. Towards the end of his life, he was elected an Honorary Life Vice-President for his long support of both the school and the Society. A later chapter outlines some of the links he maintained with many of those he had taught.

7: THE WIDER COMMUNITY

ANYONE READING ABOUT GEORGE'S COMMITMENT to CRGS could be forgiven for thinking that he would have had no time for any activities outside. They would be greatly mistaken. David Forder arrived in Colchester at the end of 1963 to take charge of the old Repertory Theatre. He said "Soon, when I was standing in my dinner jacket in the foyer one evening before a performance, as we did in those days, the House Manager nudged me. 'Mr. and Mrs. Young' she said in an awed whisper. That was the first time I saw George and Eve." He added that he "soon learnt what an outstandingly good friend George had been to the Rep. The Rep had had great days during the war and immediately after but by 1951 it was not getting the almost impossible 90% attendance it needed to survive and there were no subsidies available in those days. Therefore a meeting of supporters was held and 300 turned up. As a result the Repertory Theatre Club was formed to raise money and to give help in kind. It enrolled 600 members – more than the auditorium could hold at a time – and George was its Secretary. He did the lion's share of the work. He drafted leaflets and printed them on a small printing press he had in his attic. He stuffed leaflets tirelessly. He devised Newsletters. This continuing support enabled the Rep to survive."

In the 1970s the Mercury Theatre grew out of the old Rep and David Forder became Chief Executive. The building was funded in three equal ways; through contributions from the Arts Council, the Borough Council, and public appeal. At George's suggestion the cream of local amateur dramatic societies got together to form The Priory Players. They were so called because initially they staged open air performances in the grounds of St. Botolph's Priory. Their first aim was to raise funds to contribute to the Mercury Theatre appeal. Their inaugural production was 'A Man For All Seasons'. At the end of the final performance David Forder said he was presented with a very substantial cheque.

Barbara Pears remembers an amusing incident when they performed "The Servant of Two Masters" by Goldoni in the Priory. "George had to take over the role of the servant at very short notice. He was wonderful! However, on one evening he dashed on through a sacking curtain at the back of the stage and his wig came off. I was on stage as Beatrice and corpsed, burst into laughter, as did the whole of the audience. David Forder was in the audience that evening. After a while George said 'I think I'll do that again', went back through the sacking curtain, adjusted his wig, came through again – and carried on. What a trouper!"

The Priory Players put on shows in the Priory for some years until, as George said "the vandals drove us away". Later, as he told Jim Acheson, a Colchester firm of solicitors allowed them to produce shows in the very big back garden of the building in which they ran their business. However at the age of 92, he said "I've given up producing now but I'm still the President and go to the meetings and I did, in fact, have a brief appearance in Much Ado About Nothing, as the messenger in the first scene. I like to think that I'm still interested, and the younger people may want to stay in the society if they think, well he's been doing it all these years and he's still interested in it."

George's participation in the Priory Players was just one part of George's contribution to the theatrical life of the area. After his move to the Institute he had an opportunity to renew the interest in the Music Hall which began in his early life. Graham Smith, who joined the staff there soon after George, was himself a fine baritone and a comedian and shared George's passion for Music Hall. Graham thought it would be a good idea to put on a Christmas concert for the rest of the staff and their children. George became "the chap who introduced the numbers to begin with", the Master of Ceremonies for this. Then he got to do occasional numbers as well. When they put on the show, one of the staff who lived out in the country asked whether they could bring it to his village at Christmas time. This initiated the idea of putting on the show outside the Institute. In 1975 Graham started his Eponymous Music Hall and George rapidly became a mainstay as performer and as Chairman. Roderic Knott, who was also one of the performers, said that for the next thirty years they performed all over Essex and Suffolk, and even into Norfolk, raising many thousands of pounds for charity. He added that during this time Music Hall became Vaudeville with the Roaring Twenties, featuring many of the original cast, and even Concert Party with the Semitones, but Music Hall was always in the background and available on request.

The Roaring Twenties shows ran for a number of years but eventually ran their time. They became very large and rather unwieldy, with a cast of 22, a band of 11 and a backstage crew. They had ambitious choreography and needed regular rehearsals. So George, Graham Smith and Ken Ferris, who was Musical Director created the Phoenix Music Hall group, so named as it rose from the ashes of the Roaring Twenties shows. The Phoenix Music Hall shows featured mainly solo acts with opening and closing choruses.

The Semitones was a later development based on Little Horkesley Church Choir. The shows comprised mainly songs from West End Shows interspersed with comic numbers. George frequently appeared as a guest star and all the members of the Music Hall became occasional performers as and when invited. Invitations to perform in Village Halls, Old Peoples Homes and Church Halls came from various local groups and audiences ranged from a dozen to a couple of hundred.

Turning to George's own performances in the Music Halls and other groups, Roderic Knott, who was a fellow performer in very many of them, said "Memories abound. There was Mr. Chairman, already 80 years old, flinging himself off his chair with emotion when Sheila sang 'Don't 'ang my 'Arry' and dancing with audience members in 'Lily of Laguna'. His most loved contributions included Marriott Edgar monologues like the adventures of Albert Ramsbottom. Particularly enjoyed by audiences were 'Recumbent Posture', which he performed with different hats and different voices for each character, and his version of 'The Vicar and I'. Then there were 'Don't have any more, Mrs. Moore', 'The Green Tie on the Little Yellow God, and favourites from Rudyard Kipling's 'Barrack Room Ballads'."

George carried on performing until he was in his nineties. At the age of 91 he was named as Britain's oldest active amateur performer and presented with a trophy by the charity Counsel and Care for the Elderly. He was given the award because of his age, talent and contribution to the community. He was presented with the trophy by HRH the Duchess of Gloucester at a gala night in London. It should be noted that, in addition to all his contributions to the community and to charity described above, for many years he was also involved with editing and presenting a monthly magazine – including interviews with local people – for the Talking Newspaper for the Blind.

At the age of 92, when being taken to one of the monthly lunches he attended with a number of former students, he remarked that he had to go to St. Ives in Cambridgeshire later that week. When asked the reason he said he had been asked to go to take part in a show to entertain the "old people" there! Later that year, when being interviewed by Jim Acheson, he described this event. "Graham Smith runs a rather superior group of people who sing but they took me along to St. Ives in Cambridgeshire to do my comic acts in between to liven it up for the old folk in St. Ives. So we went to entertain them and that was my last appearance on any public stage. That was some time in July, and that indeed had rather an amusing situation because I was a little bit doubtful how my memory was going to work. So I thought I'll do one I think I know well, and then I'll sing 'Don't have any more, Mrs. Moore', because I can always do that, and that's easy, I've been singing that for years. I did my piece, and then all of a sudden I dried as I was reciting something. There was a woman sitting at a table in the audience. She went along with it because she knew it, so she went on with it and brought me back in again. I happened to have a few quid in my pocket in case they wanted me to buy raffle tickets, so I took a pound out and I put it on the little plate, which she had in front of her. I said 'Thank you very much.' The audience all thought it was a put up job and it was all very, very funny. So I got away with it, and I got away with the 'Don't have any more, Mrs. Moore', and all went well, but I don't think I'll be appearing again for a bit."

That was George's last appearance on a public stage, although he did of course live until just before his 99th birthday. He remained very active until the last year or so of his life, staying in touch with his many friends, including lunching with a group of former students once a month and hosting the annual lunch for his birthday.

In concluding this chapter about George in the wider community I can do no better than quote what David Forder said at George's funeral "George's contribution to the community in Colchester was somehow greater than the sum of its parts. He was one of the few people who made Colchester what it was, and to some extent still is. We shall all miss him deeply and treasure his memory."

The oldest hoofer in town

George is still tripping the light fantastic at 91

VETERAN thespian Major George Young still enjoys the smell of the grease paint and the roar of the crowd as he steps into the spotlight.

And at 91, he has been named the oldest active amateur performer in the region after tripping the light fantastic since he was just ten.

His work as a director and producer since the 1940s led to a starring role as chairman in the Old Time Music Hall Show.

Major Young's amazing track record as a regular stage performer has landed him the title given out by Counsel and Care, which offers help and advice for older people.

Major Young said: "Some people retire and just sit on their bottoms and do nothing but I wanted to do something to keep me busy."

He will now compete for the national title to be announced in London on Wednesday, May 29.
● Full story and more

● Young at heart – George Young, still performing at the

(1) Cutting from the Colchester Evening Gazette when George won the regional title

46

George scoops major award

A VETERAN actor proved he is 91-years young when he received a top award for his amateur performing.

Major George Young, of Plough Drive, took centre stage at a gala night in London after being named Britain's oldest active amateur performer.

He was presented with a trophy by HRH the Duchess of Gloucester and Emma Hockridge at the event.

The charity, Counsel and Care for the Elderly, chose Major Young because of his age, talent and contribution to the community.

● Centre stage – Major George Young receiving his award from the Duchess of Gloucester at a gala

(2) Cutting from the Colchester Evening Gazette when George received his national award

(3) George as Mr. Chairman or Master of Ceremonies

(4) George in one of the hats from his battered suitcase for "Recumbent Posture" monologue (photo originally published in the Colchester Evening Gazette)

(5) Another hat for "Recumbent Posture" (photo originally published in the Colchester Evening Gazette)

(6) A further hat for "Recumbent Posture" (photo originally published in the Colchester Evening Gazette)

8: GEORGE AND FRIENDSHIP

FRIENDSHIP WAS VERY IMPORTANT TO George. At the end of the interview recorded on the DVD, Jim Acheson had asked George how he would like to be remembered. George replied "I would like to be remembered, I think, as a chap who tried never to let any of my friends down, and had so many friends and made so many friends. I think I'm very proud of the number of friends I have who think I'm not a bad old soak after all."

George did indeed make very many friends both among those he taught and those with whom he came into contact in the community, whether through the theatre and music hall, the "Talking Newspaper for the Blind", even when learning Italian with what he called his "Italian chattering class". He was such an inspiration to those he taught at CRGS and was held in such high regard that many individuals remained in regular contact with him for more than sixty years. Of course he also met many at OCS events. He attended the annual Dinner and Reunion Day each year. When the Society had a Cricket Club he umpired games and his wife, Eve, organised the players' wives and girl friends to provide the teas for home matches. However some slightly more formal contacts with groups of former students started from his 80th birthday. A small group invited George and Eve to lunch to celebrate this. The following year, 1992, he said to those who had invited him "You were kind enough to invite me to a lunch last year to celebrate my birthday. This year I would like to invite you and to add a few more former students." This lunch took place in the Balkerne Restaurant at Colchester Institute and George invited some fifty of those he had taught to attend.

Thus began what became an annual event, to which George personally sent out invitations every year until his 98th birthday when his daughter, Alison, assisted him. After his death in January 2010, just before his 99th birthday, some of his friends decided to carry on the tradition. As a result Tony Golding arranged the George Young Birthday Lunch in the Balkerne Restaurant in March 2010 and I have continued to do so in subsequent years. In 2018 some forty former students attended the lunch to celebrate the 107th anniversary of his birth and to drink a glass of Merlot to his memory.

When George reached his 90th birthday Tony Golding and I asked the Headmaster if we could put on a musical celebration of this in CRGS Hall. He agreed to this. I went to lunch with George to talk about our proposal. The first thing he said was "We could do it to raise funds to go to the School Development Appeal". The second was "What do you want me to do?" While I did not really think it was at all likely, I said "Well it's for your Birthday, so you can just sit there and enjoy it!" In the event my two sons, Kevin Sharp OC and Neil Sharp OC, and daughter-in-law,

Ann Atkinson, agreed to put on a programme of songs from Opera and Operetta in the first half of the evening and George arranged for a number of his friends to perform a programme of Music Hall acts in the second half. As I had expected, he acted as Master of Ceremonies for the whole evening. This was attended by more than 100 of his friends and raised a substantial sum in donations. This money was used by the Headmaster to refurbish a room in Elyanore house as the George Young Drama Studio. As described in the next chapter, the success of this venture led to the proposal for a memorial to George a few years later.

From his time teaching at Colchester Institute George regularly lunched in the Balkerne Restaurant there on a Thursday when it was open. It was his custom to invite one of his many friends to join him on each occasion. We usually provided him with a lift, but he always insisted on paying the bill – just as he did for his annual birthday lunch. It was this generosity, where he was providing the lunch – and, usually, the wine – each year for a number of us, that caused Tony Golding to propose that a few of us who lived in the area should take him to lunch once a month during the year. This continued until he felt he was too frail to attend, at which point we decided to keep the lunches going, but every other month rather than monthly. At the time of writing these lunches still take place, with a dozen or more former students attending on each occasion. As also described in the next chapter, it was at one of these lunches that the proposal was made to set up "The Friends of George Young" to progress the raising of funds for a memorial.

(1) George at his 90th Birthday celebration as he receives the GMY Book of Tributes from David Sowter and Alan Sharp

(2) George at the 90th Birthday celebration with Ann Atkinson, Kevin Sharp OC and Neil Sharp OC

(3) George with Tony Golding and the Birthday Cake

(4) George performing with Music Hall colleagues at his 90th Birthday Celebration. From the left they are Graham Smith, Claire Short, Jim Connor, Belinda Mottram and Roderic Knott OC. The accompanist is Beryl Cowen.

(5) George with a group of OC friends at 1995 Birthday Lunch

(6) George at 1995 Birthday Lunch with John Wright and Peter Herbert

(7) George at 1995 Birthday Lunch with Peter Crafford

(8) Dave Machell presenting the caricature to George at 1995 Birthday Lunch

(9) Caricature produced by David Machell

9: THE GEORGE YOUNG BUILDING AND "THE FRIENDS OF GEORGE YOUNG"

THE OFFICIAL OPENING OF THE George Young Building took place on the evening of Thursday 27th March 2014. George's daughter, Alison, came over from her home in Paris to cut the ribbon and open the building named after her father. The ceremony was a celebration both of the new school facility and of the life of the former English and Drama schoolmaster who inspired so many of his students at CRGS 50 years and more ago. It also provided the Headmaster with an opportunity to thank all those present for their support.

The building is a magnificent venue for drama productions, music concerts, dance, lectures, exhibitions, recitals and public speaking. It is also an eye-catching addition to the school site. The foyer contains memorabilia associated with George, skilfully gathered together and presented by Laurie Holmes, School Archivist, and Liz Dodds. These include the bust by Sheila Scott formerly in the Drama Studio and the caricature produced some years ago by Dave Machell.

Students of the school put on a varied programme of entertainment for the 150 guests who attended the opening ceremony. This included recitals of Seamus Heaney poems, music performances by the Barber Shop group, the Chamber Choir and the cast of Les Misérables, speeches given by some members of the Public Speaking Society and drama from the Year 7 students preparing for a performance of Julius Caesar.

The opening of such a building is something for which George's many friends could only have dreamed when they embarked on the campaign four years earlier. It was then that Tony Golding and I decided we would run an appeal to raise funds for a memorial. All George's friends owe a great debt of gratitude to the Headmaster, Ken Jenkinson, first for his success in securing the grant to enable the building to go ahead, and second for agreeing that it should be called the George Young Building. We know that George would have been extremely proud to have such a memorial. He would also have been delighted to witness the demonstration at the opening of how the building will help to develop future students' abilities in the Performing Arts so dear to him. Both the building and its future use are great tributes to his memory.

For our part we, the Friends of George Young, were delighted that we were able to raise over £50,000 as our contribution. Raising a significant amount of money is rarely easy and many difficulties had to be overcome on the way. It is an indication of the number of friends that George made, and of the strength of feeling they had for him, that those difficulties were overcome, when it would have been easy to give up.

When George died Tony Golding and I put forward the idea of raising money for a continuing memorial at the School. Based on the support received when we had organised the event on the occasion of his 90th birthday, we indicated to the Headmaster that we were confident a significant sum could be raised for a memorial and asked him how he might use this to benefit the School. He said there was a need for a Performance Studio for Drama and Music. The money raised could go towards this, and the building could be associated with George in some way. Another possibility was to use the money to fund an appropriate bursary. The drawback with this second possibility was that, unless the fund was replenished with additional money over the years, it would soon run out. Therefore such use would not meet the object of a continuing memorial.

Shortly after this discussion with the Headmaster, Tony and I, who were both past Presidents of the Old Colcestrian Society and long serving members of its General Committee, reported at a meeting of the committee that we intended to run an appeal. However we suggested that, in view of George's long support for the School and the Society, the fact that he had been an Honorary Life Vice-President of the Society, and that the funds raised would be used to benefit the School, it might be run as a Society appeal. This was agreed and the appeal was launched officially with a document sent to all members in April 2010 and with an announcement at a Memorial Concert on Friday 23rd April (very appropriately Shakespeare's birthday). This featured Ann Atkinson (Mezzo Soprano), Kevin Sharp OC (Baritone), Members of Priory Players including Jenny Burke, Barbara Pears and John Flint, and members of Eponymous and Phoenix Music Hall Groups including Graham Smith and Roderic Knott OC.

During the next few months donations were received from a number of individuals. In order that donations could be Gift Aided where possible, these were made to CRGS Trust to be held there on behalf of the appeal. Two concerts were given by Bro Glyndwr Male Voice Choir from North Wales and soloists Ann Atkinson (Mezzo Soprano) and Kevin Sharp OC (Baritone) accompanied by Daniel Law, the first in the School Hall on Friday 22nd October 2010, the second at Dedham Church on Saturday 23rd October 2010. In addition Tony Golding arranged for copies to be made of the DVD "Memories of Major George 'Bolo' Young MC MA" and these were sold in aid of the appeal.

During the autumn it became clear that funds needed to ensure that the Performance Studio would go ahead could not be obtained from the Local Education Authority. In addition while the Headmaster still needed the building, and it remained in the School Development Plan, he did not know from where, when or even if, he would be able to secure the bulk of the necessary funds. By the end of 2010 the CRGS Trust held a total of £7800 on behalf of the appeal.

Of this over £3600 had been raised through the various events and almost £4200 came from donations. It was also apparent that, despite the fact that it was a Society Appeal, no member who had not been taught by George had made a donation and few had supported the concerts. It was indicative of this lack of support from those who had not been taught by him that even one officer of the Society, asked to buy a DVD to support the appeal, declined on the grounds that he "did not know him." In addition the Trustees of CRGS Trust were questioning whether they could hold the funds – and therefore claim the tax back on gift aided donations.

The Officers and some members of the General Committee of the Society were in favour of closing the appeal, using some of the money raised for bursaries and the balance for some permanent memorial. The view of some of those who had raised and donated the money differed. They felt that if there was a need for the building it was possible that over the next few years a source of funding would be found. At the suggestion of Ian Sutherland, I proposed that the appeal should continue with a target of £50,000 to be raised over five years to support the eventual construction of a Performance Studio for Drama and Music at the School. The Society President, John Shrimplin, explained this at the 2010 Dinner and asked members for their support. Nevertheless at the next meeting of the General Committee in January 2011 the majority were unwilling to support this proposition. They preferred to close the appeal at the figure raised to date, use £2000 of this for bursaries and the balance for a permanent memorial to George as, for example, a specially commissioned portrait or stained glass window.

During the last few years of George's life a number of those he had taught had met him for lunch once a month. When he became too frail to attend they decided to continue with the lunches, but every other month. At a lunch meeting, in late January 2011, Jim Wellerd proposed that if the General Committee were not willing to support the appeal, as proposed by John Shrimplin at the Dinner, they as "friends of George Young" should indicate that they would do so. This was put to the General Committee in writing in a letter signed by 19 former pupils including nine past Presidents of the Old Colcestrian Society. There followed a disagreement over how the funds raised up to that point should be allocated. The General Committee claimed that since the appeal had been initiated under their auspices the funds were theirs to allocate as they chose and this should be as above. The "friends" felt strongly that those who had raised it should have the major say. In addition they were convinced from their knowledge of George that he would never have approved of money raised in his memory being used on a permanent memorial, like a painting or stained glass window, that was of limited benefit to students. In order to overcome the apparent impasse and avoid the possibility of some sort of division between the "friends", who had all been members of the Society for many years and the General Committee, I made the following proposal on behalf of the "friends".

1. As from 6 April 2011, "The Friends of George Young" will take over the administration and raising of funds for the George Young Appeal.
2. Of the funds already raised, up to £2000 will be available this year to the Headmaster to allocate from "The George Fund" to students in cases of financial hardship. In future years the General Committee of the Society intends to raise an amount annually for that fund.
3. The balance of the money so far raised will stay in the George Young Appeal and will go towards the target of £50,000 for that fund to support the eventual construction of a Performance Studio.

At the next meeting of the General Committee the Society Chairman proposed that this should be agreed. This motion was carried with all but one member voting in favour. The latter said his only objection was that he felt it should remain a Society Appeal and that all the money raised to date should go to support the eventual construction of a Performance Studio at the School.

Now that the development of the appeal had passed to "The Friends of George Young", a committee was set up to manage this. It comprised Alan Sharp – Chairman, Jim Wellerd – Vice-Chairman and Secretary, Peter Herbert – Treasurer, David Sowter – Membership Secretary, Ray Lindley, who took on the task of setting up and running a 100 Club, Ian Sutherland and John Shrimplin. To assist administration a "Friends of George Young" bank account was opened and a register of supporters established. Over the next eighteen months a number of events were run and the funds increased through their net proceeds

- A lunch at Watercress Hall hosted by David and Nancy Cannon
- "Pandora" a new musical written and directed by two CRGS pupils, James Bowstead and Oliver Wood. The Friends of George Young provided financial support to the production and the Appeal benefited from the proceeds after all costs had been met.
- A Cabaret Dinner featuring Margaret Preece at the Centennial Suite at the Community Stadium on Friday 23rd March 2012.
- Concerts at the School on Friday 18th May 2012 and at Dedham Church on Saturday 19th May 2012 by the Bro Glyndwr Male Voice Choir
- Eightieth Birthday Celebration for Alan Sharp in CRGS School Hall on Saturday 8th September 2012 (donations made by guests to the appeal) Entertainment provided by Margaret Preece – soprano, Ann Atkinson – mezzo soprano, Neil Sharp OC – tenor, Kevin Sharp OC – baritone, accompanied on the piano by Colin Nicholson OC

In addition the 100 Club, managed by Ray Lindley, provided net monthly income to the appeal.

The School having applied for and gained academy status, the Headmaster subsequently obtained a government grant to enable plans for a new multi-purpose building to go ahead. However he was aware that he would also need as much money as The Friends of George Young could raise to ensure that the building was to the specification and quality desired. Originally an arbitrary target had been set of £50,000 over five years to support the eventual construction of such a building, since there was no way of knowing if and when the School would secure the greater part of the funding necessary. The original appeal had been launched in April 2010 and The Friends of George Young had assumed full responsibility for its development in April 2011. The building would now be completed by autumn 2013, just over three years since the appeal commenced and just over two years since The Friends of George Young was formed.

The fund stood at the time at £15,000 and there was now a period of 12 months, rather than three years, to try to meet the original target. However the building had become a reality. Those who doubted whether it would ever be built could now be reassured. In addition the Headmaster had generously decided to name the new building "The George Young Building". It was now time to make a major push for donations. To increase the value of those donations it was decided to seek charitable status. As a result of the experience of David Sowter this was achieved, and a "final push" for donations was launched in May 2013. As a result a cheque for £38,000 was handed to the Headmaster in September 2013. Further cheques were handed over at the official opening of the building on 27th March 2014 and on OC Reunion Day 2015, bringing the total to £50,000. In fact, including money raised directly from a talk given by James Acheson OC in the George Young Building in May 2014, the £2000 allocated earlier for bursaries and a small amount handed over when the charity was finally closed, the total raised in George's memory was just over £54,000.

Of this, some £15,000 had come from various events. David and Nancy Cannon hosted two lunches at their home and there were eight concerts and other musical performances. In addition, after the opening Jim Acheson gave a talk in the new building entitled "From the Comic Book to the Silver Screen ... Designing Superheroes for the Movies", and we were extremely grateful to him for doing so. We were greatly indebted to all those who helped make the events successful. This included all those who sold tickets for them, including in particular Doreen Massey, Peter Wright and Gill Nicholson. It included those who helped out at them e.g. Marcus Harrington ran a bar at the concerts at the School. It included all those who bought tickets and supported the various events and those who purchased the

DVD. Finally we were especially grateful to all those who performed at one or more of the various musical events. These include the Bro Glyndŵr Male Voice Choir from North Wales, Ann Atkinson, Kevin Sharp OC, Neil Sharp OC and Margaret Preece. As well as helping to boost the fund, their performances were greatly enjoyed by all the audiences.

When we set the target of £50,000 we were told we would never reach it. What is true is that we would have got nowhere near that figure without the generous donations of a very large number of individuals. The names of seventy of these are recorded in the foyer. Some are members of George's family and other friends but sixty-two are former students who were taught by George. There are as many again among the names of further donors included in a list at the end of this chapter. In a way this seems astonishing since it was over 70 years since George came to Colchester to teach at the School and over 50 years since he left. It is another tribute to him and an indication of the regard with which he was held that after so many years so many of those he taught supported the appeal. As recorded in the previous chapter, George said "I think I would like to be remembered as someone who tried never to let my friends down – and had so many friends, and made so many friends. I would like to think that my many friends will feel I was not a bad old soak after all". The success of the appeal and the George Young Building itself provide the evidence that this is indeed is how he is remembered.

Some of those who made donations in cash at the concerts or other events remain anonymous. However the following list includes the names of all those who made generous donations of varying amounts and/or contributed through membership of the 100 Club.

James Acheson
Andrew Alexander
Mike Almond
Jeff Andrews
Owen Avis
Roger Bacon
Daphne Badcock
Colin Baker
Terry Bareham
Robert Barnard
Brian Barton
Trevor Bedford
John Bennett
Roger Bruce
M. Bushall
Barry Byford
David Cannon
Tom Cannon
Harry Carlo
Paul Carr
Nigel Chapman
The Cooksey Family
Peter Cox
Alan Daldry
Peter Crafford
John de St. Jorre
David Donaldson
Derek Drew
Len Drinkell
Terry Duncombe
Keith Dyer
Peter Eaton
Peter Fenning
Michael Ferdinando
Graham Fisher
John Fisher
John Flower
David Forder
Tony Forsgate

John Francis
Stewart Francis
Tony Frost
A.S, Fulcher
Tony Gladwin
John Godden
Christine Golding
Tony Golding
David Gollifer
Macarthur Gollifer
John Gray
Alan Harper
Laurie Hemmings
Peter Herbert
John Hible
Tim Hughes
Bob Humphreys
Ken Jenkinson
Peter Kirby
Julian Lord
Dick Jackson
Clive Jenner
David Jennings
Andrew Jones
Ray Lindley
David Loshak
Douglas McMillan
Geoffrey Markham
Allen Martin
Alan Massey
Roger Mills
Andrew Moseley
Jeremy Mynott
Simon Mynott
Peter Napper
Barry Newman
David Nice
George Nicholson
Peter Norton

Grahame Page
Roy Paris
Oliver Peacock
Barbara Pears
Ian Pettitt
Derek Portsmouth
David Preddy
John Pye
John Ransom
David Richardson
Alan Robinson
Adrian Rose
Chris G. Rose
Christopher J. Rose
Alan Ross
Westley Sandford
Jack Sargent
Alan Sharp
John Shrimplin

David Smith
Michael Smith
David Sowter
Ian Sutherland
Bob Taylor
Bruce Taylor
Bryan Turner
Chris Turton
Alan Waldock
Pete Wallbridge
Charles Ward
Jim Wellerd
Gunnar Westholm
Christopher Whybrow
Jon Wiseman
John Wright
John Wyatt
Alison Young
John Young

(1) Alison Young and CRGS Headmaster Ken Jenkinson opening the George Young Building

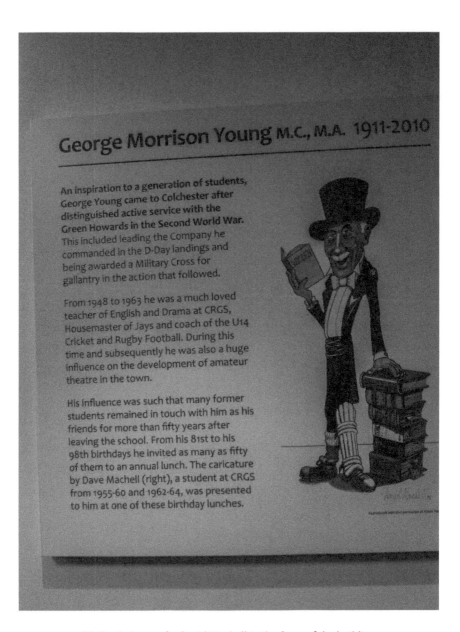

George Morrison Young M.C., M.A. 1911-2010

An inspiration to a generation of students, George Young came to Colchester after distinguished active service with the Green Howards in the Second World War. This included leading the Company he commanded in the D-Day landings and being awarded a Military Cross for gallantry in the action that followed.

From 1948 to 1963 he was a much loved teacher of English and Drama at CRGS, Housemaster of Jays and coach of the U14 Cricket and Rugby Football. During this time and subsequently he was also a huge influence on the development of amateur theatre in the town.

His influence was such that many former students remained in touch with him as his friends for more than fifty years after leaving the school. From his 81st to his 98th birthdays he invited as many as fifty of them to an annual lunch. The caricature by Dave Machell (right), a student at CRGS from 1955-60 and 1962-64, was presented to him at one of these birthday lunches.

(2) The Caricature by David Machell in the foyer of the building

(3) Bust by Sheila Scott and plaque of names of donors in the foyer

(4) The George Young Building

APPENDIX

GEORGE YOUNG'S
90TH BIRTHDAY
BOOK OF TRIBUTES

28TH MARCH 2001

Experiences with GMY,

by a fraction of his friends

XC

GMY90

These pages contain contributions to George Young's 90th Birthday Book, dated 2001. Tributes and recollections came from across the UK, sent in by friends in the area and by former students of Colchester Royal Grammar School. George received the book on-stage at the March birthday Concert, and took it home.

His daughter Alison came across it after his death in February 2010. She looked after it in Paris. Recently, when we decided to create copies of it for a wider circulation., Alison took on the task of scanning the contents page by page and emailing them to the Friends of George Young. We owe Alison a massive debt of gratitude.

Much of the content dates from 2001, but some has come in since. The plan is to add this as an appendix to Alan Sharp's new biography of George, which will be on view in the George Young Building.

We are proud to share them with you - and with posterity - in honour of a great man, an outstanding teacher who was - and still is - greatly admired and loved.

FOGY

The Friends of George Young - 2019

XCXCXCXCXCXCXCXCXCXCXCXCXCXCXCXCXCXCXCXC

Robert Barnard

When I think of George Young, I hear two voices. One is the voice all CRGS pupils heard at one time or another – in form-rooms, during rehearsals or on the playing fields. Namely, the apprentice Town Crier. The other voice was heard by fewer and it sounded quite different. It was the voice you heard when he taught Chaucer, demonstrating how it ought to sound.

'Whan that Aprill with his shour-es soo-te
The droughts of March hath perc-ed to the roo-tz'

It sounded wonderful. It sounded right. Of course, he may have been bull-shitting us the whole time (he wouldn't have been the only CRGS master doing that). The main thing, though, was that it opened doors. It made readable the apparently invincibly obscure.

When I think back to my schooldays, my overwhelming feeling is of how much I have lost. Physics: gone. Spanish: gone. Latin: virtually gone, save the declensions of nouns): Geometry and trigonometry both gone (what little there ever was).

Two things remain. The dates of monarchs and prime ministers, inculcated by Hiram Hall and exceptionally useful, so that the moment you hear the date of an event, the publication of a book or the mark on a piece of silver, you can place it in a reign: give it a context.

Then, the Chaucer – George's wonderful gift to his pupils, an enabling gift, opening up one of the funniest and most humane writers in our literature.

Of course, the other thing about George, the infuriating thing, has been his refusal to age. Around him, people wither, buildings crumble, objects obtain a patina of age, but he looks, seems and even sounds pretty much as he did back in the 5C in 1952. Something must have been stretched in the immutable laws of the human condition for this to be so. I suspect there is in George's attic at 31 Beaconsfield Avenue a painting of the handsome young George, painted in Blackpool like as not, and though this has wrinkled, become blear-eyed, gap-toothed and slightly grey, George soldiers on, hats on, bats on, acts on, just the same.

If CRGS in the 1950s is anything to go by, few schoolmasters become known by their pupils by their actual first name alone. It is therefore a sign of his great distinction – and of our great affection – that we salute, simply, **GEORGE, 90**

Bob Barnard

I'm sitting overlooking the Balkerne Gate as I write this. The Balkerne Gate has been a way of passage - in and out, entry and outgoing - for over two millennia.

George has, for us, been a gate into and out of the world of education for most of our lifetimes. By education, I don't mean the narrow curriculum of English literature. Indeed, I cannot really remember any English literature which I learned at George's feet. But, that notwithstanding, George had the greatest educational influence on me - as he had on others - of any of my mentors. Through George I entered on a whole new world of experience, and via George I emerged as a more confident person, better able to negotiate with the world around me.

'George' is a name meaning 'tiller of the soil'. Whatever he thought of us poor sods, he took us and accepted us, no matter how fertile or infertile the ground, and sowed the seed. It was up to us what we made of it. For myself, as one to whom the sporting ethos of the school was largely barren, George showed me that I had a value which did not depend on the numbers 15 or 11. Without George I should look back @ my time at CRGS as largely sterile. When I think of CRGS 1947-1955 it is of George, thank goodness, that I think.

Tom Beckwith. 2001.

72

Trevor Bedford

I arrived at Colchester Royal Grammar School, ex-India, in 1947, aged 13. The School was still recovering from World War II, staffed by retirees 'recalled to the colours'. Rationing in force, no school uniform, discipline non-existent, anarchy reigned. Messrs. Cunningham, Donson, Young et al arrived and instilled discipline and order, building on the battered traditions and infrastructure that remained.

George swept into my class, the lowest and least talented of the low, held up the famous red and black books, invited us to remain in the red and warned us, dramatic pause, never to enter the black! For the first time this callow and supremely dim youth had met a teacher able to discern in him some spark of intelligence, to fan almost-dead embers into something of a flame and to stimulate a long-dormant desire to learn.

His example, wisdom and friendship endure to this day. I remain in his debt
Trevor Bedford, CRGS 1947 – 52

- » 1954 National Service. Subaltern in Hong Kong, Korea and Japan.
- » 1956 University
- » 1959 Shell Petroleum: Management Trainee
- » 1960 Foreign Service, Hong Kong
- » 1974 Headhunted – defects to commerce
- » 1976 CEO of multinational property, food and hotel group. Chairman or Director of several other companies.
- » 1983 onward: Non-executive Director/Chairman of several companies operating in the UK, Europe, SE Asia and the USA.

Married, three children, five grandchildren. Reading, music, golf.

Have always remained in touch with George and Eve (greatly missed and so much a part of George's persona). All who were taught by him were privileged – and to become a friend, the more so.

Derek Brightwell

Although it was 52 years ago, I can still recall George's dramatic entry into my form-room in Gurney Benham. Bursting through the door and with a great flourish, he announced his name, his age and what he intended to do for/to us. What an entrance!

Half a century on, he remains a classic English gentleman, whom I continue to regard as a source of learning and inspiration.

Despite my undistinguished five and a half years as a boarder at Colchester RGS - both academically and in terms of sporting achievement (apart from minor talents for ping-pong and tennis) - George always made me feel of significance. I was invited to tea at his home: he was the first teacher to visit me after I broke my leg playing rugby; and he made a speech in the dinner hut on my last day, making much of what I had up till then regarded as a very minor contribution to the School. A welcome boost to my confidence.

With his amazing School productions of plays by such as Daviot, Shakespeare and Shaw, plus a trip to the Old Vic to see Donald Wolfit in 'Tamberlaine', George made many great works accessible and enjoyable. He introduced one to the joys of the theatre.

Thanks in large measure to the School and to teachers such as George, one has enjoyed a happy and fulfilled life - good jobs with Ford, Unilever and Bovril (where I became MD in my early 30s) - then 25 years heading my own management consultancy with some major international clients including Bermuda Tourism, and now playing the gentleman farmer with a 7-acre garden open to the public.

Thanks. George.

Derek Brightwell

CRGS 1947-52

David Cannon

It is with the greatest pleasure that I subscribe to these memoirs of George. His influence and contribution to my future during my School days are impossible to measure, but I know – along with many others – that our association with such an outstanding person has been one of the greatest advantages of our lives.

Soon after leaving, I got to know my future wife's family, unbelievably hard-working Scottish farmers whose sole aim was to work and farm 110%. We married and have lived at Fordham for nearly 48 years, raising our five children to follow the same example. We now have 13 grandchildren who look like following suit. There's a photograph on the second page.

In 1984 I became a Borough Councillor and in 1998 had the honour of being elected Mayor of Colchester. How proud I am of Colchester, of Colchester Royal Grammar School and especially proud of George Young.

My earliest recollection of George was when he first came to CRGS and became the English master for our form. A tall, spare man, very efficient. Friendly, but with an aura of mystery. There were rumours of a distinguished war service, but he never spoke of that – at least not to us, the young ones who were the most excited to hear.

Although connected to agriculture through my father being a Blacksmith, and having several relations in farming, I only became truly dedicated to that life after I read a book that George introduced to the class. It was "Farmers' Glory" by A G Street. The visions of Canada's wide open spaces were vividly described, igniting in me spark of interest, which steadily grew.

Visiting Canada six years ago with my wife, we drove right across the continent, more than 5,000 miles, readily understanding A G Street's wonderment at a horizon that goes on and on.

Here is the family picture (over the page).

Here we all are (well, most of us) protected by the brass cannons!

Nancy, my wife, Scottish daughter of a Scots farmer.

Robert, Blacksmith and Plant Hire. Three children.

Elizabeth, Antique Dealer. Married. Two children

Marie, own business, married to a farmer. Three children.

Fiona, Solicitor, married to a farmer. Three children.

Ian, Farming and a specialist woodworking business. Married. Two children.

David Cannon

Watercress Hall

Fordham

Colchester   CRGS

1944-49

GEORGE

Exactly half a century ago you were teaching me English literature in that very special environment of 5R. It took a gifted teacher to interest some of the denizens of that class!

I can *still* hear your rendition of the confrontation between Pip and the convict. What life you gave to the book. Another set text was Julius Caesar and I was delighted to be able to see you taking a part in an open air production of that very play just a few years back.

Inevitably, your lessons were not confined to the set topic [an understatement!] and one gained some idea of what it meant to have first hand experience of war- its pathos, its comradeship and even its moments of humour.

Later, when I was House Captain of 'Js', it was your advice on leadership and man management and your knowledge of rugby football tactics which I remember.

Like myself in my teaching career, I know you have gained great pleasure from keeping in touch with former pupils over the years but you greatly surpass me in your amazing memory of names, faces and characters.

Thanks for everything George.

Harry Carlo

Paul Carr CRGS 1949-57

Only fifty-two years on do I realise what a young man you were in 1949, George.

Paul Carr with Jennings and Bennett, fellow Boarders

No wonder you were wont to say, 'Come out here, *boy*!'

English in 4C and 5S...

C+ for me for six successive terms – and only you could find all six permutations of the words, "quite, usually and good." I wish I had remembered that in my short spell as a teacher.

Highlights?

Swapping sugar for butter in the boarding house kitchen during rationing. Mrs Elam floating through the kitchen in her nightie. Midnight feasts with Matron.

Other highlights? Start with a 'lowlight'. Never getting as many 'A' marks as Musset. L

Swimming! And of course, *the Plays, the Plays*. I am not including Physics – enjoying that came very much later. 'Bread and butter, bread and butter,' as Victor Borg would say.

You commissioned me to design a set for Hamlet based on the Mermaid and on seeing my sketch (below) you said, 'I'll buy that, Paul.' Later on, you took us to the West End to see Alastair Sim in a comedy.

We fondly imagined you liked our company. Now, I realise we were right! And having us round to tea with Mrs Young and so many other social activities, you were being far more than an English teacher to generations of boys.

"I'll buy that, Paul."

A Song for George March 2001
(To the tune of 'Sorrento')

There was once an English master
who made us all run so much faster
on the playing fields of Colchester.
The Royal school in Essex County

In classroom, field or cupboard stationery,
or in Restoration comedy
and as well in Shakespeare's tragedy,
George gave all of us the will *to be*

Ourselves in every situation,
as if we were to lead the nation
and *not to be* in degredation,
in detention in 5C.

There are other stories plenty,
of Green Howards when he's twenty
the hat routine and Holloway's poetry ,
all when George was in his eighties.

Not just in his classes
that George all else surpasses
so raise your glasses
now that George is ninety. *Paul Carr.*

At school.... Swimming captain 54-57,
2nd XV rugby. Three A levels.
57-59, Active service, Malaya.
59-62, Nottingham University, Physics.
62-82, Senior research physicist ICI.
85-99, Research Fellow in polymer physics,
Leeds University.
Church warden, Holy Trinity Dacre.
Roles with Summerbridge Players:
Mr. Soppitt in 'When we were Married',
The Undertaker in 'Oliver', The
husband in 'After Magritte'
Amatuer artist with some sales.
Married to Maureen with 7 children,19 grandchildren.

Much of this must be due to CRGS and your
good self George, especially and surprisingly
the drama. So are many of the friendships that
have been renewed and strengthened by your
hospitality. Thank you.

††

Simon Cox

"I remember it as if it were yesterday". First week, first form, tall man enters form-room, fixes boys with a stare; barks and growls for several minutes without pause. It took only a few seconds to get the message – "Don't mess with me and we'll get on fine." We got on fine. Even now, I can recite most of the opening speech in King Henry V (Oh! for a muse of fire ...) which George set us as homework.

As an enthusiastic, if modestly talented sportsman, I clearly recall three moments of gratefully received praise from George. Two sixes struck in a house match against Parr's and a crunching tackle in my first game for the first XV each produced a stentorian, "Yes!" from the watching master.

George taught me to play badminton, using boarders like Michael Norris and me to make up the staff foursomes in Hall in the evenings.

In a roundabout way, George found me a wife! Pat Young played Maria in Twelfth Night and I did her make-up. We met again in Ye Olde Cheshire Cheese in London. It will soon be our 36th anniversary, which we hope to celebrate with our son Jeremy, our daughter Hannah and our granddaughters Rachel and Annette.

Like numerous others, I think of George with a mixture of admiration, affection, gratitude and tremendous respect. He remains a great character and has made the world a better place.

Simon Cox

Simon Cox, Colchester RGS 1953-61. School Captain 1960-61.
General Practitioner, Clacton-on-Sea. President, Colchester Medical Society for the year 2000. President, Essex Bird Watching Society.

This tribute was typed by Jim Donson's daughter Margaret – my admirable secretary and friend for many years.

††

David Donaldson

My first recollection of George Young is of him striding zestfully – almost, one might say, erupting – into Upper Fifth's form room off the Hall. Having arrived at his desk, he turned to face us, a spare, moustachioed figure, and barked:

'My name is Young, George Young. I'm thirty-eight years old and I was a Major in the Army. I got the Military Cross for capturing a German jam factory. Now, to poetry and 'Sorearse and Rustibum' to you but 'Sohrab and Rustum' to the examiners!'

It is hardly surprising that several lines of that poem are still imprinted on my memory!

By the end of that inspiring first lesson from George, he had made such an impression on me that I presumed to ask him to become attached to School House (shortly afterwards to be renamed Shaw-Jeffrey's). He agreed, and it became greatly to the benefit of all members of School House, and myself in particular for my remaining years at CRGS.

George was also instrumental in getting me on stage for at least two of his School plays. If I remember aright, I had a small part in Richard of Bordeaux and then, when Michael Bailey succumbed to mumps three days before the opening night of Henry V, George had the unenviable task of turning me from playing a Welsh courtier (with a Scottish accent) into an English king (with a Scottish accent). A great challenge for us both, and great fun.

Posterity might care to record that seven years later I married the girl from the County High School cast as my mother-in-law in the play!

Derek Drew (CRGS 1944-50)

Without getting maudlin about it, what can you sensibly say about someone who has changed your life? I was a miserable misfit in the first and second forms, scooped with brighter friends from our council estate Junior by the 1944 Butler Act. Always 34th out of a class of 34, I threw in the towel after my father's death and stayed at home. An enquiring letter from the school secretary, arriving by happy chance on a day my mother was not working, ended three shameful, agonising months. Undeserved sympathy from avuncular Head Arthur Fletcher persuaded me to stay on and go back a year. Without ever shining academically, I made up a little of the lost time, especially when Fortune smiled on us all with the intake of enthusiastic young masters returning from war. Leading spirit in that breath of fresh air was George Young.

Form-mate John Shrimplin has already recorded that historic first meeting of what must have been 3A in what had been the Art Room, and the initial warning issued to possible transgressors. John may have forgotten – or perhaps not been able to notice from his seat – that the new master's dignity was somewhat dented by the regrettable fact that two buttons of his fly were undone!

That year, George Young turned grubby, dog-eared, close-printed copies of Treasure Island, Great Expectations and Kidnapped into gold. How lucky we were to have to study these classics and how lucky to have them interpreted by a Master in every sense of the word.

There followed drama that lifted us in imagination out of the ordinary into sombre Scottish castles and French courts, building character, promoting discipline equal to any to be found on the cricket or rugger fields.

I was a member of that small privileged team of baby-sitters at – was it 31? – Beaconsfield Avenue where Eve Young was always so gracious – and made sure there was sufficient comfort food for the evening. I don't recall little Alison troubling the happy hour at all!

George Young introduced me to the music of words and I was fortunate enough to capture enough of their magic to make them my stock-in-trade and a passport to life's finer things. After 45 years in newspapers and still a working journo, I owe George, as I suspect do the majority of the subscribers to this book of tributes, more than any words can express.

We look forward – not too soon, because we're all cracking on, God knows! – to celebrating the centenary!

Derek Drew, contd. (A tragi-comic reprise)

The post-war Forties were years of real austerity and Parents' Day called for a George Young production of The Scottish Play stripped down to its juiciest bits. Presented on a stage bare of all but essential furniture, the action was – well, suitably enthusiastic.

Came the dramatic moment the bloodied ghost of Banquo joined the feast: the moment the maddened Macbeth let the cup fall from his lip – and from his nerveless fingers. Seconds seemed like hours as the silver goblet, revealing itself as a cut-down milk tin, rolled and rolled inexorably toward the edge of the raked stage, dropped five foot to the floor with a clang and sped with added velocity halfway up the aisle between the astonished groundlings.

Mums and mummers convulsed in laughter.

George, in Cecil B. De Mille mode, cried something on the lines of, 'Cut! Let's enjoy the moment!'

He carried the day, if not the can. After all, as someone once said, the play's the thing.

Reader – I was that insane thane!

Peter Eaton

Those who remember the School as it was during and immediately after the Second World War will doubtless recall the masters and school-mistresses who taught us. Many had come out of retirement to replace younger teachers who were in the armed forces.

However competent and well-intentioned they were, their own early exposure to education had been during the reign of Queen Victoria. This was reflected in their practice.

The return of the younger brigade on demobilisation was a revelation – and the arrival of George Young in particular was a breath of fresh air.

Peter R. Eaton, CRGS 1941-52, Harrogate, North Yorkshire 2001.

Nicholas Elam

"Through the wood, and through the wood
And through the wood it ran.
And though 'twas but a wee, wee thing
It killed a muckle man"
[Dixit G M Young – see below]

George awakened my interest in words. He knew the meanings of prolepsis, disquisitional, philoprogenitive (which I wrongly believed he invented). I caught him out once, with 'cynosure' – but only briefly, since it was a condition to which we both aspired.

Since all will remember most of the things I remember, I choose a memory only a few will have shared: George playing at the Staff Badminton Club, to which a handful of senior Boys were invited by its presiding genius, Miss Dorothy Stanyon.

Unsurprisingly, George's badminton style was dramatic. A matter of sudden, staccato bursts of energy, accomplished with systematised stamping and gestural pyrotechnics, crowned with hieratic growls and shrieks. His scoring shots were limited in scope and number, but devastating when they actually suited what the opposition had delivered. A particular speciality was the fierce, sharp-wristed smash of an irresolute, middle-court, middle-height service or return of service, deserving the kill it received.

Needless to say, George's badminton was not a drama without words. At the start of this piece, I included a quotation (from a ballad?), one of George's catchphrases that came out whenever the shuttle hit a racquet's wood and a false shot had to be declared. It is etched in my mind and has come out, unbidden, whenever a false note has been sounded in a negotiation – with a bewildering and generally discomfiting effect on the opposition.

Of course, there was also mischievousness. At moments of ludic satisfaction, George could not resist the temptation to announce the score in a carefully modulated Lowland Scots accent calculated to cause the most exquisite pain of embarrassment to the young prefects present, for its pin pointedly accurate rendering of the voice of Alec Thom, Head of PT (an ever-present, along with his wife). Mr Thom's badminton was not as talented as his masterly backstroke in the swimming pool. George's Truncheon stroke was less effective than his badminton, it should be added in fairness.

"Foorrtin,' theirrtin,' wun dune!"

It began all of fifty years ago. It seems like yesterday. The memorable is never banal. Thank you, George.

Nick

Peter Fenning

An early memory of George is a distinguished looking teacher in a flowing gown. Having never seen a teacher wearing a gown one was slightly fearful but George quickly put new boys at ease - he became a friend.

Peter Fenning 1951

At G.C.E. 'O' Levels I failed English Literature but on arriving back in the Autumn term to join 6 S' I was ambushed by George after morning assembly. With a smile he said "I see that _we_ failed English Literature and I will be putting you in for a re-sit in December – tuition will take place after school on Tuesdays and Thursdays". I sailed through the re-sit with a good mark.

Through George's influence I gained an interest in stage management, sizing and painting screens, costing props and was stage manager for one of his productions. Leading up to this production George arranged for two boys plus himself to visit Bernard Miles who was putting together the London Mermaid Theatre.

George 1952

We visited Bernard Miles at his Hampstead home and received his words of wisdom. Later George took us to Wyndhams Theatre and up 'in the gods' we watched Tyrone Power in 'Arms and the Man', all at George's personal expense.

Another occasion on which George showed his lack, or perhaps rejection, of fad or political correctness, and spoke his mind was when Colchester Rep staged Samuel Beckett's 'Waiting for Godot'. After sitting through several hours of a man ranting in a dustbin George was approached by a local dignitary who commented on the real significance of the play. George's retirt was that he preferred Shakespeare anyday.

Another example of George's ability to inspire and spread enthusiasm, not only to the Arts sixth form, but to us 'Boffins' in the science block was to involve you in charitable works. Just before 'A' Levels in 1957 he requested my presence to organise a Tombola stand at the Hospital fête. I attribute my later success in technical sales to George's instructions on the art of parting customers from their money.

It is difficult to summarize the education which George imparted to us but it could be said that he is a school master who never had to raise his voice or hand to a pupil.

Peter Fenning, C.R.G.S. 1950-57, Sixth Form Science, University of Nottingham, Honours Degree in Geology, Physics and Maths.
Director, Earth Science Systems Ltd., Kimpton, Herts. – Geophysicist
Honorary research Fellow in Civil & Environmental Engineering at the University of Edinburgh
Chartered Geologist

" Una gita a Venezia " 10/2000.

- George enjoying a quiet drink in
St. Mark's Square. Another trip with
" Gli Italianisti "

George reminded me again of the beauty and wit of
the great BARD, how much we owed to those who
drove back the NAZI terror and most importantly
what it is to be a charming and fully paid up
member of the human race. His presence in our
little Italian Circle has been central to its
continuation and enjoyment over the past five years.
I look forward to many more evenings spent with
my favourite 'novantenne'. A te Giorgio
Buon Compleanno.

Bob Fisher - formerly 'Period'
Manager at Colchester Institute,
Italophile, drama and film
enthusiast who came late in life
to appreciate George Young, his
wit, modesty and great sense of
humour.

Ann and Tony Gladwin

Over the past few years, George, I've related to you some of my favourite memories of CRGS – of David Wigley, in 1C, and his, "Qui, tres posh!", of myself, in 4C, receiving the appellation, "Chump", by dear Hiram Hall (only rescinded after I'd won a history scholarship to Oxford!), of Ralph Curry's heroic 'rescue' of Snelling, in 5C.

But what are my favourite memories of yourself? There are, oh, so many.

Here are just two.

As a nervous 1st former, in 1C, and an ex North St. Primary School 1st XI footballer, trying to come to terms with Rugby Football (as you always crisply called it), I hurled myself suicidally, following your injunction to 'tackle low', at the concrete knee and toecaps of the opposition. On one occasion, during the 1C/1G grudge match I arose dazed after an encounter with a 7-stone Jonah Lomu. At this point, you laid a hand on my shoulder and said to the assembled players, "We've never before awarded a Tackling Bar to a 1st former, but we're thinking of making an exception in the case of this young man".

How proud you made me feel.

Then, much later, in your form 4C....that Anglo-Saxon class featuring Messrs Van der Straaten, Dupont and Schomberg, in the C stream that, for me, always seemed to begin with Angier, Bareham, and conclude with Whyard, Wicks.

It was your custom, after the lunch break, to put in a brief appearance in the classroom to ensure all was in order before you dismissed yourself to your duties. Not much was said, just a proprietorial glance around the room, and you were off.

However, on this occasion something seemed amiss. You were clearly discomforted in some way. We sensed it.

You couldn't contain yourself any longer. "It's bloody ridiculous", you protested, "how can anyone claim that a Sesterce is worth one and eightpence!?" Indeed, how could anyone know the then present worth of a quarter of a Denarius? It was not as if the Romans could easily buy a ticket to the cinema, or a couple of pints of milk.

And yet, the more interesting question for me was, who had put forward this proposition? Surely not one of the classics masters. Arthur Brown was far too sensible. Nor could it be dear Leggy Lamb, for the lunch break would not have afforded enough time for him to articulate his arguments. Baron Casey? Possibly.

Who was it, George? I've always wondered.

So many memories.....

Of always hoping that you, George, would be the deputising teacher if one's own teacher was away. With any luck you might read us a piece of Dickens, or introduce us to some other author. You might talk a little about your war experiences – not too much, and I think we are now of an age to appreciate how difficult that can be for a soldier, but we schoolboys loved it.

And your habit of concluding any conversation about localities with your sharply-rendered version of, "Towns, small islands, domus and rus!"

You taught us and we learned from you. You made it fun.

Ann and I now treasure your friendship.

Ann and Tony Gladwin

" .... the whining schoolboy, with his satchel,
and shining morning face, creeping like snail
Unwillingly to school "

" .... Then a soldier,
Full of strange oaths."

" .... and Then the justice (????)
In fair round belly ...."

GEORGE — in some small way this Book of
memories may serve to remind you of the
respect and affection in which you are
held by those of us, fortunate enough,
as schoolboys, to have received your
teaching and guidance.

Tony Goodwin

Tony Gladwin

"... And then the whining schoolboy, with his satchel

And shining morning face, creeping like snail

Unwillingly to school.

"... Then a soldier,

Full of strange oaths, and bearded like the pard...

"... And then the justice,

In fair round belly with good capon lined..."

GEORGE – in some small way this book of memories may serve to remind you of the respect and affection in which you are held by those of us fortunate enough, as schoolboys, to have received your teaching and guidance.

Tony Gladwin

Quotations are from Shakespeare's 'As You Like It' describing the Seven Ages of Man.

Tony Golding (CRGS 1946-1954)

Not for the first time do I appreciate the fact that I was born a Catholic, because that was the reason I first came into close contact with George. In Upper II in those far-off days it was decreed that from above that we were excluded from RE lessons. George came into one such class being conducted by Mr Bennett and asked if there were any Catholics who might help in the Book Room.

Thus began an enjoyable, fruitful and happy association that lasted through all my years at CRGS and continues right up to the present day.

Mike Hurley and I spent many hours with George in the Book Room. He trusted us to hand out the books, paper, pencils, etc., and to sell other items. We felt privileged, especially when George shared a bit of gossip about some of the other teachers. Having been born in Yorkshire, I had retained quite a bit of the accent and George never missed an opportunity to imitate me. Yet this never once annoyed me, as he only did this when describing the latest success of 'J's' house, which seemed to occur far too often. However, Dugards did win the cricket in my time!

When I look back at my English lessons with George, I recollect liberating Sicily, kissing the Headman of every village, taking part in the Normandy landings and generally winning the War – all spiced up with lots of advice on how to live one's life. 'If you want to teach, be sure and marry someone with money, as I did'.

At the same time, he instilled in us a love of literature without us realising it. He introduced us to the classics, including Shakespeare in particular. And who can forget his reading of 'Great Expectations'?

Similarly, he transmitted his love of cricket and rugby. His enthusiasm and his knack of explaining the intricacies of the various games were infectious. George was never short of words and his accounts of our junior cricket games in his 'Colt Magazine' were always worth reading.

George cared for 'the whole boy.' He was interested in all of us and this showed from the very beginning. Because of this, he is vastly appreciated by Old Colcestrians all over the world. I have been lucky, living in Colchester, to meet him regularly.

David Gollifer 1946-51

Taught English by George from Form IIIc to 6Si. His grammar lessons were often interspersed and exemplified by Rugby football analogies, including blackboard diagrams on, say, the importance of running to the corner to score. Along with reminiscences of World War II and the loud, continuous noise of the artillery.

Tackling Badge 1949   *Form Master 4S 1949*

George awarded me a tackling badge for bringing down P.R. Eaton when he was away on the right wing in a house rugger match. I also had a decent report from him one term.

> All students remember the particular teachers who made a lasting impression on them. For me, that teacher is George Young. He was the favourite of many, well respected and in a class of his own.

With George as my Mentor, I soon learned to appreciate the subtleties and depth of William Shakespeare's 'Julius Caesar' and to enjoy Joseph Conrad's, 'The Rover,' both set texts for the School Certificate English Literature exams.

His lessons were always rich in content, delivery and enjoyment. I remember him telling us that the word, 'spiv' would not always be in common usage as it had been in the 1940s. And he was right. Thank you, George, for being at CRGS when I was there.

David E. Gollifer

I retired after 38 years working as a tropical agronomist in developing countries with the Ministry of Overseas Development. Currently Hon. Sec. of Great Bentley WEA.

Earliest memory – George & his burly henchman (?) Packmore in the Book Room

Most vivid memory – George directing 'The Devil's Disciple', and 'the Scottish Play', c 1962 with Tim Hughes, Geoff Henshall et al. – seen from back stage as a member of the crew.

"WHEN I WANT THE WOOD TO MOVE, I'LL TELL YOU"

What you gave me, George, is a love and understanding of the English language. Apart from the sheer joy of watching you relish it as you read it aloud, you could & did teach how to use it for clarity, effect and humour, especially through 'FOSPS', as you called them – bathos, litotes and the rest – a daily pleasure for one whose life has been nothing but words!

"I shall live & die a judge" – it is for others to complete it, or not, as they see fit!

You distinguished once the shades of meaning between 'Teacher' & 'schoolmaster'. Bless you, George – what an example of both! Cliff Gypps

GODFREY GYPPS
CRGS 1959/66
PRESIDENT OCS 1997.

XCXCXCXCXCXCXCXCXCXCXCXCXCXCXCXCXCXCXCXCXCXCXCXCXCXCXCXCXCXCXCXCXCXCXC
XCXCXCXCXCXCXCXCXCXCXCXCXCXCXCXCXCXCXCXCXCXCXCXCXCXCXCXCXCXCXCXCXCXCXC

Alan Harper

George Young at C R G S late 40s and 50s

George was my form master from September 1951 until July 1952. He taught me English and English Literature from 1949 until 1955 when I left CRGS to do two years National Service. His classes were always lively affairs with many personal anecdotes from George mainly about Rugby Football or Cricket, occasionally about War Service. I always remember him saying that he made a point of carrying a rifle instead of a pistol believing that to carry a pistol might persuade the opposition that he was an officer and worth shooting first!

Lessons when George read to us from the set books were always a joy. He read "The Gun" by C S Forester, in the forth year, the year before it was our GCE set book. Those of us who read ahead in the book wondered how he was going to carry off the name of the peasant hero, Jorge, but he was prepared and produced a wonderfully Spanish " Hor je' ". I well remember his other readings and in particular his love of Shakespeare's plays and the way he made them come to life. Last week we went to the Mercury to see "Arms and the Man" another memory of George's English Literature lessons.

I never got any better than the second game at Rugby and I played tennis for the school instead of cricket. My last Summer at school I was drafted into "The Rest" team to play Cricket against Shaw Jeffrey's only recently renamed from "School" House and again the champion house. "The Rest" innings disintegrated and, on that day, I was left holding the tail together and scoring some runs. We managed to salvage a draw and when we came off George, who was J's Housemaster said " Well done, but you are a fool". He obviously felt that I should be playing cricket and not wasting my time at tennis.

My time at CRGS shaped the future of my life and gave me the confidence and inner belief to deal with life and people and to tackle problems without fears or worries. I owe a great deal to the school for that and particularly to George who was one of the main inspirational examples.

I am proud now to have a grandson at CRGS.

Alan Harper
CRGS 1948 to 1955 Harsnetts

Brian Hutton (CRGS 1948-53)

It is almost impossible to find suitable words to express what George Young meant to me and the influence he has had on my life.

It was through his example, with that of G.V. Fancourt that I decided to become a schoolmaster – a decision I never regretted. Like G.V.F., I qualified in Geography and based my teaching on his and George's because both were far ahead of their time in the methods they used.

I think George joined the staff in January 1948. I cannot recall coming into contact with him until the September of that year when we, Form 4S, were fortunate enough to have him for English. There were many reasons why he never seemed to have a problem with discipline. For one thing, his lessons were always interesting and informative, and there was always a very relaxed atmosphere. Also, he took an interest in us as individuals, spent countless hours in extra-curricular activities and was never afraid to delegate responsibilities.

What highlights can I recall? The open-air production of Henry V (with David Donaldson's famous ad-lib). St. Joan, with Anne Hardy from CCHS. Hamlet, which I returned to see after I had left. Which one was it that the local paper suggested must have been directed by somebody from London?

His devotion to Shaw-Jeffries' House was suitably rewarded when, in my final year, we won all the sports trophies. George was not Housemaster (that was W.J. Hughes) but it was his inspiration and the countless hours he devoted to coaching that made this possible.

It was indeed a great privilege to be at CRGS, greatly enhanced by one's contact with GMY.

One final thought. To help us with our English Lit. revision in '5S, George produced a crossword. If my memory serves me correctly, one of the clues was:

"*Ecclesiastical metamorphosis occurred to this taciturn agricultural worker.*"

(For answer, see 'A Dutch Picture' by Longfellow).

I wonder what would be a suitable clue to lead us to George?

Brian Hutton, 157 Yardley Fields Road, Birmingham B33 8RP

14-iii-2001

Assembler's clue proposal: 'Great elder of Royal Grammar education, from the beginnings'

David Jennings

11 Rowland Avenue, Manchester M20 3QY
1st March 2001

Dear Mr Young,

I see no reason why you should remember me, any more than I remember the majority of my own former pupils. And yet, a few years ago, there was a slogan, 'You never forget a good teacher.' The occasion of your 90th birthday seems an excellent time to thank you for being just that.

You were my 4C form-master almost 50 years ago, in 1952-53. You read with us, as I recall, 'The Rivals'. 'Henry V' and (I seem to recall) a preliminary skirmish with 'Macbeth' in preparation for O-levels the following year with Mr Ralph Curry.

At all events, you took us to see 'Macbeth' in London, on a reconstruction of an Elizabethan stage somewhere in the City. I still remember being briefly taken aback when Lady Macbeth was reading that letter, looking for all the world like an animated portrait of Elizabeth I. More trips to London theatres followed: Gwen Ffrangcon Davies and Esme Perry in 'The Cherry Orchard' at the Lyric, Hammersmith, plus at least two visits to the 'Old Vic 'to see 'Much Ado...' and 'Richard III' (the latter with Robert Helpmann). All these, together with your own productions at School and the Colchester Rep, got my theatre-going off to a fine start. It is a pleasure that has stayed with me ever since.

I appeared in only one of your School productions, doubling up as Reynaldo and the English Ambassador in 'Hamlet'. That has been the entirety of my acting career – except that any schoolteacher 'acts' in the form room.

They were good days, my days at CRGS. For a boy from a working-class home they were a wonderful introduction to a world of learning, culture and ideas. I feel lucky to have been at the School at that time, when there did not seem to be the pressures which assail the young nowadays.

I am very sorry I cannot join you on the 23rd March. Do you still reply, when asked how old you are, 'I am not old; I'm Young!'? I do hope so. I certainly wish you a very happy birthday, and offer again my thanks for the education in which you played a leading part.

With best wishes from
David Jennings

Roderic Knott (contributed in 2018)

When George left CRGS he went to Colchester Institute where he developed acquaintances with its restaurant ('Chefs') and with Graham Smith who shared his passion for Music Hall. The restaurant link was to be a source of gratitude for us with its superb cooking. (*Note 1*)

As a result, in 1975, when Graham started his Eponymous Music Hall, George rapidly became a mainstay as performer and Chairman. I had met Graham through the Institute's Music department where we appeared in operas, and thus I met George again, many years after he had told me never to try to appear on a stage! Meanwhile, I had appeared in plays and pantomimes and sung in all kinds of concerts (*Note 2*). I liked an audience but was not good at sticking to a script. Ad-libbing was not encouraged in CRGS productions. However, for the next thirty years we performed all over Essex and Suffolk, raising many thousands of pounds for charity. Music Hall became Vaudeville with the Roaring Twenties and even Concert Party with the Semitones, but Music Hall was always in the background on request.

Memories abound. There he was, Mr. Chairman, 80 years of age, flinging himself off his chair with emotion when Sheila sang "Don't 'ang my 'Arry" and dancing with the audience to "Lily of Laguna".

His most loved contributions included Marriott Edgar monologues such as the adventures of Albert Ramsbottom, particularly "The Recumbent Posture", with different hats and voices for each character, and his versions of "The Vicar and I", "Don't 'ave any more, Mrs. Moore", "The Green Tie on the Little Yellow God" and favourites from Rudyard Kipling's "Barrack Room Ballads".

He truly deserved the accolade of the award for the oldest active performer at the age of 91, and he continued for another couple of years.

A true Gentleman!

Assembler's notes – by David Sowter

"Gratitude" because even after 50 years the fabulous Institute Restaurant remains the venue for the annual George Young Birthday gathering in March. George was born on 28th March 1911. He passed on in February 2010 at the age of 98.

Roderic does not mention the time he profoundly stirred our emotions with his rendering of 'See them pass by!' (Le Rêve Passe) to an audience including many Parisians who had accompanied George's daughter Alison to the 90th birthday concert. Roddy enchanted the French and all nationalities present with the range and melody of his true tenor voice.

"See them pass by,	*Les voyez-vous,*
Their hussars, their dragoons, their guardsmen ...	*leurs hussards, leurs dragons, leur Garde,..*

Michael Leatherdale (CRGS 1946-54)

By its nature, by its title (Book of Tributes), this book is intended as an encomium[Note 1].

Well, sycophancy was not a concept taught me at CRGS, so I shall spoil the fun. Mr. Young (I still hesitate to call him 'George') failed me in so many ways.

He let me leave school an innocent, leaving it to Her Majesty's Army to introduce me to the joys of alcohol, tobacco and debauchery. To give him his due, he did cast me as Macbeth, knowing that I, in a kilt, would have to embrace the lovely Helena. But if that was his attempt at sex education, it was ineffectual.

Mr. Young instilled in me a love for the English language, its grammar and usage. Well, all that's done is to make me insufferable, irritating those closest to me with my huffing and puffing over split infinitives, missing 't's (Wha' a pi'y) and others' inability to differentiate between the nominative and accusative ('Me and Peter went to Twickenham'; 'Between you and I'). Had it not been for Mr. Young, damn it, I could have been a fan of EastEnders.

He taught me a love for English literature too. A fat lot of use that's been! It helps with the Times Crossword and pub quizzes but, come on, Sir, how have Shakespeare and Marlowe, Dickens and Greene contributed to my income? They could have – I might have won a million on television even – had he had the foresight to interest me in pop music and film stars. But he totally ignored these important matters without which life seems incomplete.

Then there's sport. Apart from encouraging me to upset my mother by returning home twice a week battered, bruised and muddied by rugby matches, Mr. Young did me the disservice of introducing me to Lord's Cricket Ground. He took a coachload of us to see a performance of Macbeth in a London theatre. Instead of returning us immediately to Colchester, he ordered the driver to St. John's Wood where a curious, purple-jacketed boy stared in wonder at a scene unequalled in the World. As a result, over the last fifty years (an MCC member for twenty of them) I've wasted many an hour of my invaluable time at Lord's, watching the game with past heroes like Bill Edrich, Len Hutton and David Gower., slurping whisky or beer in one or other of the Pavilion bars: lunches in marquees, cream teas in the sun. And I blame you, Mr. Young, for half a century of this torment.

So, dear George, me and Hazel (sic) congratulate you on your achievement and look forward to your next annual pilgrimage to Harrogate when we can relive old days over steak and kidney pie and a bottle of claret[Note 2].

Assembler's comments:

Note 1: (First para) Here we see a prime example of Michael's self-avowed insufferableness in matters of language. He uses the word 'encomium'. I had to look it up but I shall save you the trouble of doing so by stating what I discovered. Encomium means 'high commendation: a eulogy'.

Note 2: (Final para) One suspects that George would have preferred a bottle (or two) of Burgundy.

Linda and Gerald Lees

I originally got to know George and Eve through the Italian circle about 14 years ago and they became good friends to Gerald and me. When he lost Eve, I was very impressed at the way George took an interest in cooking and was soon able to create the most wonderful meals, marinating meat to make the most delicious casseroles, baking his own bread and turning his home-grown fruit and vegetables into fabulous puddings and soups. We attended Italian lessons together and often shared a pizza afterwards and then this developed to a few of us meeting once a week at The Cricketers where we chatted informally in Italian much to the amusement of other customers! It's been wonderful to share those and many other happy times together. George is greatly interested in people from all walks of life and he has always made me feel important. He is such an impressive man and I value his friendship greatly.
Linda Lees

Fun with George includes trips to Turin, Milan, and Venice; watching him perform recitations with many hats or in clerical garb; and many an evening, at home or restaurant, where George's anecdotes or memories are never just recollections but always have a point. His comments on politics, education, rugby and cricket are always worth listening to carefully. I feel grateful to George for his friendship towards Linda and me, and admire him for all he does, above all the behind-the-scenes help and support he gives to friends and neighbours. George has lived through some of the dark times of recent history but these haven't dimmed his faith in the decency of people when they are decently treated. In that, he's a wonderful fuori serie! Viva Giorgio!
Gerald Lees

Allen Martin

Rosencrantz without Guildenstern ... and without the hose!

" A sponge my lord?"

With lines like that no wonder we got chosen for our legs!!

Subject ENGLISH   General: Nobody Advy Ord.   Name MARTIN A.D.

Grade   C

SUBJECT REPORT

His work has been interesting.

Initials
A—Exceptionally Good. B—Above Average. C—Average. D—Below Average. E—Definitely Weak.

There are several more like this, showing an infinite capacity for laconic re-working of a tried and tested theme!

Reasons to be thankful

- enjoying reading essays on motor racing
- Saturday afternoons watching me trying to keep my kit clean of mud
- Saturdays given up and spent travelling away with callow youths
- seeing the young as people
- the book store
- the under 14's - the shorts and the legs that mostly all went in the same direction at the same time
- the tea and biscuits in Jays diner - paid for by you
- Eve and the costumes
- the joy of successful collaboration - in class, on the stage and on the pitch
- the mastering of frustration - most of the time
- doing something worthwhile well
- valuing the "Mog" Morgans equally with the T.G.Barehams - unless they were Jays, of course
- keeping things in perspective - even if it should have been the best soliloquy in the world
- theatre in the classroom - sometimes drama, often mellow but never quite farce
- the two Australian soldiers - the numerous one-arm flute players
- the friendship over the years
- sharing some wine - well, quite a lot really
- agreeing that mostly "they're all a bunch of bloody clowns!"
- lots of laughter
- ...and especially the yarns

Fondest regards from the " handsome Midge" and his family.

John Meadowcroft

" ...... A big tribute is due to all those who gave such industrious assistance behind the scenes, above all to the anonymous producer whose identity puzzles reporters but who is still the indefatigable Mr Young".

This extract from The Colcestrian on the 1959 School Production of Twelfth Night brings back very happy memories of my involvement as a member of the make-up team, which included fellow boarders P.T. Hart, J.S. Gibbs, S.Cox, T.F.N. Johnson and N.J. Heightman.

*　　　*　　　*　　　*　　　*

Shaw Jeffery's 1955-56

The great encouragement and enthusiasm provided by George Young, in his own inimitable style, was undoubtedly one of the main reasons that my House, Shaw Jeffery's, was so successful in sporting competitions against the other Houses. "J's" won the Singer Cup in each of the years I was at CRGS.

*　　　*　　　*　　　*　　　*

The values and experiences I gained at CRGS have immeasurably helped me in my career as a Chartered Accountant and in my wider life with family and friends. I feel most privileged to have attended the school, of which George Young was such an essential part.

John Meadowcroft
CRGS 1952-59

Gerald Nason

But I'm an artist really—or so I tell myself;
so one last memory; when I had my first
one-man show in Colchester who was there
from C.R.G.S? Yes, you George and though you
were a bit baffled you wished me all the
best, as usual, and I really appreciated
that. So here's an orig. for you c.1955
together with one of the latest. Hope
you're not baffled ... still. And for you
George, all the best and happy
memories ...

Ged

1949-55 C.R.G.S.

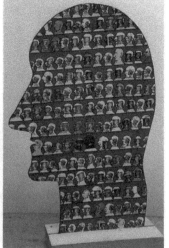

1938	Born Colchester
1955-59	Colchester School of Art
1959-62	Royal College of Art (Stained Glass Department)
1962	Editor of 'Ark' (R.C.A. magazine)
1962-65	Editor (with Ken Baynes) of 'Number'
1963-67	Assistant Editor, 'Architectural Review'

1967 to present Artist, Art Teacher and Writer, living in
                                        Laxfield, Suffolk.
Regular exhibitions in London, Essex and Suffolk (Colchester,
Ipswich, Sudbury, Hadleigh, Yoxford, Halesworth, Snape and
Laxfield), and Germany

3CHURCHWALK
Gerald Nason
LAXFIELD SUFFOLK IP138DL

104

Gerald Nason II

for George

Gerald Nason III

Earliest memory? Easy: those legs! As some wit wrote in the School mag... "Nobbly, nobbly Barney's knees were "... But in this instance the knees were yours and I'd never seen the like. No, you weren't teaching English at the time, merely rugby... However I made it to the 1st $\overline{XV}$ (previo page) so maybe they were an inspiration... the knees I mean. And from what I hear, they're still going strong! May they continue for years...

presents

MACBETH

by

WILLIAM SHAKESPEARE

March 23rd - 27th, 1954

Was I Third Soldier or Fifth? The programme lists us only as "Soldiers etc." b came the command "Now near enough your leafy screens throw down!" a Tonih Hughes and I hurled our withered leafless bits of branch down wit such a clatter that, "And show like those you are".. was barely heard... And what were we? A real self-conscious bunch of spotty adolescents with orange faces and arms and bloody uncomfortable helmets! Hell, but I loved it! And knees notwithstanding. there's no one example of your influence on my later life that's stronger than that fanatical effort you put into the drama. Thank you George, you got me hooke for life....! If it hadn't been for you there'd be none of this $\mathbb{K}$

George Nicholson

"The wind! the wind has changed!"

I wagged that pennant in "St. Joan" CRGS 195?.

I was also the back-room boy who George brought in from the cold, to smell the greasepaint.

Maybe not "Laertes in Macbeth" 1955, but his lighting technician who then went on to operational sub-contracts with the BBC and ITV Broadcast Companies.

I spent my school rugby days as an undistinguished member of the Third XV at CRGS.

However in the late 1950's, haunted by the sound of GMY's whistle and his accompanying exhortations, I became the top scoring wing threequarter for Maldon First XV.

Forty six years after leaving CRGS, despite having seen him once during that time, the one Master who remains vividly in my mind, is

George Young.

It seemed that whatever I was involved in, George was there, guiding and enthusing.

Above all George made you believe that your own achievement was important to him personally.

Thank you George for seeding and nurturing both my cultural and physical development.

Married 35 years. 2.0 children.

Boarder C.R.G.S. 1949-1955
Epic film maker with John F. Bennett
Advanced Scuba Diver.
Retarded Skier
Retired Technical Services Manager for
GEC EO Systems Group.

Many Happy Returns George.
George Nicholson — GEORGE NICHOLSON

The Pears

A very Happy 90th Birthday
to you George - a dear friend-
story-teller extraordinaire -
dedicated teacher - genius of
the "triple word score" and
an illustrious actor.
To appear on stage with you
George reminded one of the
utterance "Never act with
animals or children" and I
add...or George Young.
You simply shine!

With much love from
Barbara - Geoff, John
and Lynn Pears
and Alexander X

Bruce Polley

Fenn Cottage
Lower Road
Grundisburgh
Woodbridge
Suffolk IP13 6UQ

21st. March 2001

Dear David Souter,

I have returned from several weeks away to find that George Young's 90th is upon us. George did not teach me much, but there are memories of the David Donaldson Henry V and of a very tall dark rugby ref. at Park Road. I have not completed a sheet as George may not ever remember me, but I do send him my
best wishes

Bruce Polley
1946 – 1953 (Dyson)

Modest cheque enclosed.

S. A. Read

MACBETH 1961

Hello George;

My earliest memories of your influence are through the school plays. No you were never able to draw out my hidden thespian talents, but being a boarder I had plenty of time to help off stage.

I remember one humorous occasion when you were calling out the register.
" Is composition Read present?"
You had to explain to a bemused class that my initials were SA (essay).

I was a lost cause at school as far as english language was concerned.
However your exceptional teaching skills raised my standard from D- to C+ enabling me to pass at GCE.

CRGS provided me with a good education and prepared me well for a successful career in civil engineering. I am a director with WS Atkins and a Fellow of the Institution of Civil Engineers.
I have to smile when I correct our graduates training reports and essays for syntax and spelling errors. I think back to the young schoolboy who could only manage D- in english language.

Having been a boarder its ironic that I now live in Colchester with my wife Janet.

George, its always a joy when we meet and you give me your cheery greeting; " Hello Read, how are you?".

1956 – 1963

Alan Sharp

GEORGE

You remarked that we met first when you joined our table for lunch. My earliest significant memory is of you selecting for special mention, to my great surprise, an essay I had written following a visit to the Rep. to see Macbeth. This was mainly because I had commented on the effect of omitting a small, apparently inconsequential scene. Later, in the VIth, it was one of the great privileges of taking subsidiary English and History to receive short periods of individual tuition from you and A.F. Hall. Your sonorous reading of Chaucer - not to mention vivid explanations of meaning e.g. "a shiten shepherd" remain in the memory.

Outside the classroom what I remember most is your great enthusiasm for your Under 14s, and some "gems" in the reports in "The Colcestrian". Just who were the batsmen who "stoppeth one of three" and who "on this occasion, as on others, had a good off-stump as off-stumps go - and, as off-stumps go, his went"? I respected greatly, too, your energy in support of Shaw-Jeffrey's, even if it was not directly in my interests as House Captain of Dugard's from 1948 to 1951!

In the early years post school I and other O.C. cricketers remember with gratitude the support given by Eve and by you to us and our wives and girl-friends. In more recent times, happily for me, our contact has been more frequent, with many enjoyable conversations on cricket, rugby football, politics and other topics. I think I can now say with some confidence I have overcome the obstacles of being too old to be a member of your Under 14s, of being in Dugard's and not Shaw-Jeffrey's, of not being a keen "thespian". Fortunately my sons have inherited the appropriate gene from their maternal grandfather, so they are able to assist us in helping to celebrate your 90th birthday in an appropriate fashion.

Your energy, enthusiasm and joie de vivre are an example to us all.

From a now retired management consultant and occasional author (your tuition paid off!)

Alan

ALAN SHARP

CRGS 1943-1951

111

John Shrimplin

1948: Form 3A – English Lesson: Enter a tall man – a very tall man – from Blackpool. He says in a commanding voice, "I have in my right hand a little red book and in my left hand a little black book. Anyone who crosses me will be remembered for ever in the red book."

Who would dare risk the continuing wrath of such a man? I cannot even remember how the black book was to be used. But then he held the class in rapture as he read aloud, "Great Expectations," acting each part and vividly bringing Dickens' book to life. I can still hear his rendition of Joe Gargery shaking his head and saying, **"Pip, old chap."**

The concern shown by Joe for Pip is akin to the humanity that George showed to his pupils and latterly to his increasingly elderly former pupils. It was never enough for George to teach English to the inept (such as myself). His purpose and nature is to enrich lives.

His invitations to boarders to tea and scones provided a modicum of home comfort to lighten the greyness of their dormitories.

Henry V 1951 will be remembered by all who served in her. Bit players like myself (Bardolph) enjoyed the experience of performing to an audience and basking in the developing romance between Henry and Katherine. And yet, the play served another purpose. It opened the School to the outside in a way quite different from sporting activities, which to my mind was beneficial to everyone. Furthermore, the CRGS Book Room brought George into contact with every boy in the School. There can be few who attended during his tenure that do not remember him.

CRGS played a major part in my life (as a boarder) until I left in 1952. My only link with Colchester was the School, but moving to Hampshire and later to the USA resulted in my losing direct contact. I still received the OCS newsletters and in one of them I read a claim from George that could remember everyone he had taught, I put this to the test by writing to him c/o the OCS. He passed the test with flying colours, even reminding me of things I had forgotten. Now I might not remember all those who ever taught me but **"George, old chap!"** I certainly remember you.

My "flair" was in maths, so in my case George drew the short straw and very short it was!

Two attempts were necessary to meet the English Language requirement for University entrance. I left School with great expectations.

Over the years, I have found that while science was my field, ideas and insights have to be communicated in English (additional languages are quite beyond me!) So thanks for English and Communication.

SHRIMPLIN John Steven, *b* 6 May 1934, *s* of the late John Reginald Shrimplin and Kathleen (nee Stevens).

m Hazel Baughen: two *s* .Educ: WWII evacuee. CRGS (1945-52 – Boarder 1948-52). Kings College, University of London (B.Sc. Mathematics). FRAeS. Joined RAE, Farnborough 1956. Defence Operations Analysis, 1966. Joint Services Staff College 1970. Weapons Dept., RAe, 1971. Defence Staff, British Embassy, Washington 1972.

Asst. Dir. Future Air Systems, MOD PE 1974. Asst. Chief Scientist, RAF 1978. Head of Weapons Dept., RAe 1981.

Deputy Head British Defence Staff, Washington 1985. Director of Defence Science 1988. Deputy Director General, British National Space Centre 1991. UK representative European Space Policy Committee, 1994.Member, European Space Agency Appeals Board, 1999. Address: 7 Clarewood Drive, Camberley, Surrey GU15 3TE.

David Smith

Taken in 1951 at the Festival of Britain! I think it was that year that I sang in Mr Fisher's choir (The Agincourt Song and The Silver Swan) at the outdoor Henry V. It was so cold one evening that soup was served in the interval! It was my introduction to your school productions, George, and what an introduction, seeing that great production night after night! I was behind the scenes for a number of your productions, providing music directly from gramophone records - once a post-horn sounded after it had been mentioned on stage! I have wonderful memories of Macbeth, Hamlet, Julius Caesar and She Stoops to Conquer.

Early Memory:
George Young's
Henry the Fifth

George - I am so grateful to you for passing on to me your enthusiasms for literature, drama and games, all lifelong interests for me. Thanks also for the advice you gave my parents when you and they were discussing my future! I have always appreciated your advice and wisdom - as a pupil, as a colleague when I taught at CRGS in the year before I went to university, and as a friend in subsequent visits to Colchester. And, of course, I learned a great deal about schoolmastering from you!

David Smith (CRGS 1950-1958). Schoolmaster Winchester College (1965 - 2001) teaching Chemistry and, occasionally, English (!) and History. Housemaster (Sergeant's) (1973 - 1988).

From a
postcard
of about
1940

Winchester College

Finally - a quotation!

' More: .... Why not be a teacher? You'd be
          a fine teacher. Perhaps, a great one.

  Rich :   And if I was who would know it?

  More :   You, your pupils, your friends, God. ,
           Not a bad public that.

You were a great teacher and schoolmaster George - and
you are a great friend.
All best wishes and congratulations on your
90th Birthday. With gratitude and with affection,
David

115

David Sowter (added in 2019)

I was incompetent to contribute a tribute in 2001 because I had nothing to say that could do George justice, nor match the plaudits of those who did contribute. I was abashed.

Now I feel able to declare that this lovely man was a legendary schoolmaster, a courageous soldier and a considerable showman. In a word, a hero.

There is ample evidence in the Alan Sharp book pages to support the first two contentions.

As for showmanship, I recollect his stage presence at The Priory Players, where his eyes regularly flashed towards the audience to see how they were enjoying him.

The tale of him joining the pupils' lunch table on his first day also inclines me to think that his motive was to differentiate himself from the crowd and win popularity among the students – not for self-aggrandisement, but to do a better job.

Some of the wartime tales recounted to James Acheson stretch belief, but since I never heard George speak false I declaim that he meant every word. He gave to German prisoners; he rescued a wounded British ranker: he promoted disobedient Private; the bullet in his tin of bully beef did end up 1mm from killing him: the 88mm shell that matched that escape, did stop 1mm from his aorta. Did he know what a millimetre looked like? In 1943? Still dubious? Well, remember this **is** George Young we are talking about! We all have our failings and foibles. His were pure entertainment – and miniscule by comparison with his great qualities and achievements.

George often says how lucky he was. We are lucky to have known him and to have had that benefit.

1956, when I'd helped him 'point' the brickwork at No. 31, Beaconsfield Avenue he gave me a bottle of Chateau La Tour du Pin Figeac 1953 from his cellar. I was 17. We'd been listening to the Ashes Test as we worked, and heard Jim Laker's 19th wicket. That called for a glass of chilled Chablis each.

I suppose I may have been a favourite. And yet I wonder how many other boys George made feel the same. Dozens. Scores. Hundreds! Me, a boarder from a council house in Dagenham with an unappealing accent? In 1984 I breached that bottle of claret and breathed its finesse. A miracle.

When I was 15 in 1953 Eve Young knitted me a sleeveless green V-neck. A very aunt-like gesture. I suspect she felt I was lacking in the casual side of the wardrobe. So cool.

By this time I was articulating fairly well – well enough for interview at Cambridge (Trinity College) in 1959 following National Service where I was the camp Dracula* in Germany. But back to that pullover. When it began to unravel during my 5th Form year I gritted my teeth and took it back to Eve. No problem. A bit of darning and all was well again! Phew! Later on, George and Eve came to tea in Trinity and I think they were rather impressed by the crust-free cucumber sandwiches. Ah! The advantages of a good Education!

*Note: I was indeed the camp Dracula in Germany. The film had been shown at our camp Kinema and given us nightmares.

I would don a black balaclava, a cloak and some fangs and roam the forested camp at night. Trained British soldiers would run away in blind panic. Once, hah! I stuck my grinning skull in at the urinals window. Nobody stayed to finish!

Charles Ward

Many congratulations, George, on your 90th birthday. It is not given to many to achieve the status of nonagenarian, and perhaps your longevity recommends us all to a busy life spent in the service of others. I consider myself privileged to have known you for nearly 50 years now, as a teacher, colleague, mentor and friend.

I joined CRGS in September, 1950, and older friends from Mile End were telling me to get into George Young's form 'because he's a super bloke,' totally ignoring the fact that I could have no influence at all on the situation!' Indeed, it was not till 1953-54 that I 'managed to get into' 4C when you were to be my form master and teacher for English. However, having been allocated to J's House, I had already benefited considerably from 'The Colonel's' influence. You took your House duties very seriously, making boys glad to belong and eager to be part of competitive ethos – especially those with sporting skills. No surprise, then, that J's dominated the inter-house competitions during the 50s, thanks to your enthusiastic encouragement and guidance. Equally impressive was the gift you had of getting to know the names of the boys, who felt themselves to be the special individuals they were to you.

That year in 4C you inspired in me an interest in Shakespeare. We studied 'Macbeth' and that 'boring old bard' took on many new dimensions. School plays were appreciated much more thoroughly now – I remember especially the imaginative production of 'Henry V' in Sholand and, later, 'Hamlet' with Terry Bareham in the title role. What a 'tour de force' that was!

I still feel sad that as School Captain, I did not take a part in the 1958 production.

Your determination to live life to the full is an example that we lesser mortals can only admire. As the French say, 'Vous avez une santé de fer.'!

Wendy joins me in wishing you continuing good health. Many thanks, George.

P.S. I do not suppose that recognising the pupils in the photographs will offer much of a challenge!

SCHOOL U.15 XV
(several of the above were in 4c)

"J's" SENIOR XV 1956-7

Lightning Source UK Ltd.
Milton Keynes UK
UKHW020312150720
366524UK00003B/5